D0204467

THE

GREAT MEDICINE
THAT CONQUERS
CLINGING TO THE
NOTION OF REALITY

Shechen Gyaltsap Pema Namgyal

THE
GREAT MEDICINE THAT CONQUERS CLINGING TO THE NOTION OF REALITY

Steps in Meditation on the Enlightened Mind

Shechen Rabjam
Jigme Chokyi Senge

Shechen Gyaltsap
Pema Namgyal

Foreword by MATTHIEU RICARD

Shambhala Publications, Inc.
Horticultural Hall
300 Massachusetts Avenue
Boston, Massachusetts 02115
www.shambhala.com

9 8 7 6 5 4 3 2 1

First Edition

Printed in the United States of America

♾ This edition is printed on acid-free paper that meets
the American National Standards Institute Z39.48 Standard.

Distributed in the United States by Random House, Inc.,
and in Canada by Random House of Canada Ltd

Designed by Lora Zorian

Library of Congress Cataloging-in-Publication Data

Shechen Rabjam Jigme Chokyi Senge, 1966—
The great medicine that conquers clinging to the notion
of reality: steps in meditation on the enlightened mind /
Shechen Rabjam Jigme Chokyi Senge, Shechen Gyaltsap
Pema Namgyal; foreword by Matthieu Ricard.
p.   cm.
Includes bibliographical references.
ISBN: 978-1-59030-440-2 (alk. paper)
1. Meditation—Buddhism. 2. Padma-rnam-rgyal,
Ze-chen Rgyal-tshab. Byan chub kyi sems bsgom
pa'i rim pa bdag 'dzin 'joms pa'i sman chen.
I. Padma-rnam-rgyal, Ze-chen Rgyal-tshab.
Byang chub kyi sems bsgom pa'i rim pa bdag 'dzin
'joms pa'i sman chen. English.
II. Title.
BQ5602.S54 2007
294.3'444—dc22
2006102598

Contents

CONTENTS

Foreword

R abjam Rinpoche, the abbot of Shechen Monastery where I have lived for the last twenty years, often says that when he was a young child he considered Dilgo Khyentse Rinpoche as a very kind grandfather. As he grew up, he began to think of him as his spiritual teacher. Once he began his studies, he realized that Khyentse Rinpoche embodied all the qualities of an authentic master as described in the scriptures. Rabjam Rinpoche was nurtured in all aspects of his life by this extraordinary human being, and he has dedicated his life to fulfilling his beloved teacher's vision, perpetuating his teachings, and now caring for the young reincarnation of Khyentse Rinpoche with the utmost love and concern.

There was no one more precious to Dilgo Khyentse than his first root teacher, Shechen Gyaltsap Pema Namgyal. He referred to him not by his personal name, but as *kadrinchen,* which means "the very kind one." Thirty years after Khyentse Rinpoche fled Tibet into exile, someone brought him a volume of Shechen Gyaltsap's in-depth teachings on the fundamentals of Buddhist practice (*ngondro triyig*), which was thought to have been lost. As he received it, Khyentse Rinpoche put it on his head with tears in his eyes and said, "This is more valuable than all the gold on earth."

In the following years, more volumes of Shechen Gyaltsap's writings were found and brought to Nepal. Among them was a collection of pieces of spiritual advice that included *The Great Medicine That Conquers Clinging to the Notion of Reality*, a concise, profound, and elegant elucidation of the relative and absolute *bodhichitta*, or "enlightened mind." It is this text that Shechen Rabjam Rinpoche has chosen as the subject for this book.

Every teacher has his own particular way of holding and passing on the authentic transmission of his spiritual lineage. Shechen Rabjam Rinpoche's teachings stand out as particularly moving in their simplicity and genuineness. He speaks from his heart in a simple, unpretentious, yet powerful way through which the reader can experience time and again the all-embracing presence of the most compassionate and boundlessly wise teacher to whom Rabjam Rinpoche dedicated his life.

Matthieu Ricard

Acknowledgments

This book is based on talks I gave on Shechen Gyaltsap's inspiring root text during the first Shechen International Seminar in Bodhgaya, India, in 2000. Additional material was added from the talks I gave in 2002 at the New York and San Francisco Shambhala centers.

I would like to express my sincere appreciation to all those who helped to make this book possible. Thank you to Matthieu Ricard for his oral translations of all the talks, for his translation of the root text, and for his guidance at every stage of the project. I am especially grateful to Ani Jinba Palmo for her dedicated word-for-word translation of the original tapes. Many thanks also to Lucy Needham for transcribing the original translation, to Sally Williams for her helpful corrections, and to Michael Tweed for his insightful editing.

My special gratitude goes to Vivian Kurz, our project manager, for her editorial assistance and her essential role in shaping the book. I am thankful to Deborah Schoeberlein for her careful attention and copy editing; to Meg Frederico for her suggestions; and to Khenpo Yeshe Gyeltsen for providing the headings for the root text, which were translated by Sean Price. Finally, all my appreciation goes to the monks of Shechen Monastery in Bodhgaya for helping to organize our annual seminars.

Introduction

I gave this commentary in Bodhgaya, India, during our annual Shechen International Seminar. Every year we invite various disciples of Dilgo Khyentse Rinpoche[1] to teach in Bodhgaya in order to give students the opportunity to listen, practice, and reflect on the teachings in this extraordinary place. According to the Mahayana tradition, Bodhgaya is not only the place where Buddha Shakyamuni achieved enlightenment, but also where all one thousand buddhas of this fortunate kalpa have achieved and will achieve enlightenment. We conduct our annual seminars there because practicing the Dharma, making offerings and prostrations, and doing circumambulations in this holy place is incredibly meaningful.

The Buddha's teachings are like medicine: they can cure us of the grave illness of afflictive emotions and ignorance. By fully understanding the power of the teachings, we will develop great respect for them and consequently for the one who taught them, Shakyamuni Buddha. The Buddha was born, lived, and taught in India. Thus, the people of Tibet have great respect and reverence for India. They often speak of it as the "supreme" or "exalted" land.

Among all of the Buddhist sites in India, Tibetans particularly respect Bodhgaya, where the Buddha achieved enlightenment. The name of this place, *Vajrasana*, means "Diamond

Throne." All of the various forms of Buddhist philosophy and practice originated in the Bodhgaya region. In particular, Buddhist teachings spread to Tibet from the great university of Nalanda.

To the ordinary eye, Bodhgaya may appear to be a dirty place, full of garbage and not especially pleasant. But when we consider that it represents the seat of the Buddha's enlightenment, Bodhgaya takes on an altogether different dimension.

Our experience of a place can change according to our view. Before leaving Tibet, my grandfather, Dilgo Khyentse Rinpoche and his family visited Samye, the location of the first monastery in Tibet, built by Padmasambhava, Shantarakshita, and the king Trisong Detsen. During this visit, Khyentse Rinpoche's youngest daughter made full prostrations around the monastery. There was dust, garbage, urine, and excrement everywhere. In spite of this, she steadily made prostrations, circumambulating the entire monastery.

After some time, Khyentse Rinpoche asked her, "Don't you find it difficult to do prostrations here? Don't you feel disgusted?" She replied, "When I think that Guru Rinpoche[2] actually visited this place and that the ground on which I am doing prostrations is the very place his precious feet touched, I feel as if he just walked by, and that the earth is still warm with his footprints. I don't feel or notice anything else." She had developed pure vision. Similarly, we too can come to see Bodhgaya with purity.

Before giving any teaching, Khyentse Rinpoche always recited the following words in a flowing voice, as if chanting a prayer:

> All sentient beings without exception, whose number
> is as vast and limitless as space, and who have been
> our kind parents in the past, aspire to happiness and
> wish to avoid suffering. Yet, afflicted by ignorance and

mental poisons, they ignore the causes of happiness. Contradicting their aspirations with their actions, they suffer from all kinds of torments in samsaric existence. They are like blind people abandoned in the middle of a desert. When they were our kind mothers, they gave us life, provided us with food, clothing, protection, and education. Seeing their unhappy condition now, we cannot help but feel great compassion. Yet the mere feeling of compassion is not enough; we must actually do something to free them from suffering. Now that we have obtained a human existence and met a spiritual teacher, it is time to progress toward enlightenment solely for their benefit.

I took these words for granted and did not pay much attention to their meaning. But now I realize that through these few sentences he expressed the quintessence of the Buddhist path and all the main points of the practice. These sentences also set a direction for our minds.

When he said, "All sentient beings without exception strive toward happiness," he did not refer only to Dharma practitioners, but rather to all sentient beings. All living beings strive to be happy and content. Take the example of a businessman who ceaselessly works to increase his wealth, believing that it will bring comfort and a good, easy life. In short, he believes his business will bring about what he imagines to be happiness. Likewise, politicians who struggle to get positions of power think that such power will bring happiness. Engaging in the practice of Dharma is no different; we too expect to achieve some kind of satisfaction. This is the very reason we go to teachers and read books. I am sure no one is reading this book out of a wish to increase his or her suffering.

Despite our desire for happiness, we easily lose track of the real purpose of our activities, getting bogged down by the very methods we thought would bring us what we want. So although a businessman tries to achieve a good and happy life by increasing his wealth, he often gets trapped in the processes of making money. Day in and day out, he is completely preoccupied with acquiring, conserving, and expanding his worth. After many years, his hair turns white and he dies while in the midst of his sole preoccupation—making money—while having completely lost sight of his initial goal, which was to find happiness.

Dharma practitioners also can lose sight of their goal. We get involved in many different kinds of practices. But do we always remember the goal of the path while in the midst of these practices? Do we lose sight of our aim to eliminate suffering and its causes while obtaining unchanging wisdom and compassion?

THE NATURE OF SUFFERING

In order to embark on this quest toward authentic and ultimate well-being, we need to examine the actual nature of suffering. There are two main types of suffering. One includes suffering that comes from outer conditions, such as poverty, sickness, natural catastrophes, wars, and so forth. The other comes from within; these inner sufferings are the products of our own mind. Although we can occasionally remedy or improve the outer sufferings quite easily, our control over them always remains limited.

In contrast, the Buddha's teachings show us how we can learn to change our inner suffering by counteracting the various afflictive emotions. The inner sufferings—the torments of the mind—arise from our destructive emotions and egoistic self-cherishing. The literal meaning of *Dharma* is "amending" or "transforming," and it refers to amending or transforming these inner mental poisons. It is said that there are twenty-one thousand sections of teachings devoted to counteracting anger, twenty-one thousand devoted to eradicating desire and attachment, twenty-one thousand devoted to dispelling mental confusion, and twenty-one thousand to breaking free of the subtle aspects of those three poisons.

Despite the clarity of the teachings, we often lose sight of this essential aim of eradicating mental poisons and self-clinging. In fact, instead of eliminating those poisons, we often end up increasing them. For example, people who practice the Dharma have a tendency to gather together and organize themselves. They create institutions, Dharma centers, and monasteries that can quickly become vehicles for proclaiming their self-importance: "We are this. We are that. We are Nyingma (or Kagyu or Sakya or Gelug)!" People within these institutions nominate someone to be president, secretary, and treasurer. These officials can easily become proud of their titles, and their activities gradually come to be at odds with their original purpose.

This is true everywhere. In the Tibetan world, we build monasteries intending to provide suitable environments in which to study and practice the Dharma. However, monasteries often become busy places where people compete for power and fame. Instead of decreasing the mental afflictions, they fuel self-importance and poisonous thoughts. Consequently, practitioners forget why they built the monasteries in the first place. Some of the great teachers of the past, such as Patrul Rinpoche,[3] often scolded their students and reminded them of the true purpose of practice, telling them that they were missing the point and not actually practicing the essence of the Dharma.

In ordinary life, we are under the power of afflictive emotions such as self-importance, anger, and desire. We have no control over these emotions, so they torment us and we suffer. We are their slaves, which is unpleasant. The purpose of the Dharma is to reverse that situation and to help us master the negative emotions—self-cherishing, pride, desire, anger and hatred—that enslave us. Being a master is much better than being a slave. Do not lose sight of this essential point: The aim of the Dharma is to get rid of disturbing emotions, and this is the only way to attain true happiness. Everyone wants what is best for him or her; nobody wants to be hurt or unhappy. If you want to be kind to yourself, practice the Dharma and free yourself from the inner sufferings and their causes.

THE FIVE PERFECTIONS

When receiving Dharma teachings, prepare yourself to get the most out of what you read or hear. First, generate the right motivation and attitude, then adopt the right conduct and behavior. *Bodhichitta*, or "enlightened mind," is the necessary motivation for receiving these teachings and putting them into practice. Bodhichitta is the precious attitude that you will work to perfect yourself and achieve buddhahood in order to help deliver all sentient beings from suffering.

The correct way to receive teachings is to avoid certain defects that would otherwise prevent us from understanding the teachings and putting them into practice. There are three defects to be avoided, and we can use the analogy of a bowl or empty vessel to explain them. The first defect is to be like a bowl that is turned upside down; no matter how much nectar is poured, not a single drop can go into it. We are like upside-down bowls when we do not pay attention to what the teacher is saying.

The second defect is to be like a bowl with holes pierced in the bottom: nectar passes through as fast as it goes in. We retain neither the words nor the meaning of the teachings when we do not listen attentively, letting everything go in one ear and out the other.

The third defect is to be like a bowl that contains poison. The poison will contaminate whatever liquid is poured into the bowl, and even a pure liquid will become poisonous because the bowl itself is poisoned. We are like this when we listen to the teachings with our mind filled with mental poisons or negative thoughts. In this situation, the teachings will not be of benefit.

Just as there are three types of defects that can hinder a person from receiving the teachings, there are five ways in which a person can fail to properly retain the teachings:

1. You retain the meaning but not the words and therefore miss something important.
2. You retain the words, but since you do not grasp their meaning, you miss something important.
3. You retain neither the words nor their meaning and therefore do not get anything from them.
4. You recollect both but misinterpret them.
5. You mix up the sequence of the teachings, thereby losing their logic and proliferating wrong ideas.

Avoid these three defects and five incorrect ways of retaining the teachings at all costs.

There are also five perfect conditions for receiving teachings:

1. The perfect place, such as Bodhgaya where the Buddha achieved enlightenment
2. The perfect teacher, exemplified by the Buddha, who accumulated all the conditions of merit and wisdom necessary to achieve ultimate enlightenment and thus became like a skillful physician who could free other beings from sufferings
3. The perfect teachings, meaning those that act like medicine to cure the sicknesses of afflictive emotions and mental poisons while eradicating their root cause, ignorance (in this case, the teachings composed by Shechen Gyaltsap Pema Namgyal)
4. The perfect disciples, who include all of the Buddha's disciples, arhats, and bodhisattvas, as well as fellow sangha members
5. The perfect time, or the fortunate kalpa when a buddha appeared and gave teachings that are still available

At present all of these circumstances have come together and enabled you to receive these teachings under the best possible conditions. Therefore, as you read, generate a sense of appreciation and joy at finding the perfect conditions to receive these teachings.

ROOT TEXT

THE GREAT MEDICINE THAT CONQUERS CLINGING TO THE NOTION OF REALITY

Steps in Meditation on the Enlightened Mind

SHECHEN GYALTSAP PEMA NAMGYAL

Namo Guru Buddha Bodhisattva
Homage to the gurus, Buddhas, and bodhisattvas!

I bow to all the masters
Who have attained supreme primordial liberation
And out of compassion remain here,
Dredging the depths of samsara.

I will speak a little about how to destroy one's
    clinging to the notion of reality
With the great medicine, bodhichitta,
The essence of the Mahayana path,
The road travelled by all the buddhas and
    bodhisattvas.

Keep this in mind when in dire straits
Upon the vast plain of clinging to life's appearances,
Surrounded by your enemies—the obscuring
    emotions—
You are about to be robbed of the supreme wealth—
    virtue.

All phenomena remain in the expanse
Of beginningless time;
Since this is the case,
All sentient beings can achieve nirvana.

Just as there is perfectly clear water
Within the earth,
Within the obscuring emotions,
There is great primordial wisdom.

The sutras that elucidate emptiness,
And all the words spoken by the Victorious Ones,
Speak of getting rid of the obscuring emotions.

Buddha-nature is immaculate.
It is profound, serene, unfabricated suchness,
An uncompounded expanse of luminosity;
Nonarising, unceasing, primordial peace,
Spontaneously present nirvana.

Just as sesame oil pervades sesame seeds,
The essence of the tathagatas
Is primordially present and inseparable from
The basic state of all beings.

Obscured by the deluded notions of subject
    and object,
Shrouded in the cocoon of the three habitual
    tendencies,

Like a treasure lying hidden in a poor man's house,
This nature remains unrecognized.

Obscuring emotions and wrong actions
Cause sufferings to fall upon us like rain.
Since beginningless time you have roamed
On the immense plain of existence, which is
   apparent yet unreal.
Alas! Such is the power of ignorance and karma.

Having fully prostrated
At the lotus feet of an authentic master,
You should cleanse the stains of ego-clinging
With the nectar of his instructions.

Now that you have at last obtained
This free, privileged human birth,
Which is so hard to find and so meaningful,
It is worthwhile to transform your being in solitude
Without being attached to this life,
Which is of such small importance.

Amid the clouds of impermanence and illusion
The lightning of life dances:
Are you sure you won't die tomorrow?
Death is unavoidable, so practice the Dharma!

Since beginningless time
In the prison of existence,
You have endured the punishment of the threefold
   suffering.
Yet you remain unconcerned—rotten heart!
Now is the time to conquer the citadel of great bliss.

Happiness and suffering are manifestations of
   karma.

You cannot escape the law of cause and effect,
So the Victorious One has said.
Knowing this, discriminate carefully:
Avoid evil deeds; accomplish virtuous acts.

Rely upon the undeceiving embodiment of all
    refuges:
The unexcelled Three Jewels.
Just hearing their names
Shatters the city of existence.

Who is more shameless in this world
Than one who abandons to samsara's ocean of
    suffering
All the mothers who have tenderly cared for him
    since beginningless time
And instead strives toward the peace of a solitary
    nirvana?

For countless kalpas,
Those with sublime intelligence and their heirs,
Have investigated and seen with their mighty
    wisdom
That precious bodhichitta alone is of major benefit.

If, among all the paths to the ultimate goal,
You tread this one and open
The treasury of the twofold aim,
What other witness will you need?

Following either of the two traditions,
Generate bodhichitta as a vow and as an action;
Learn its precepts, the detailed and the concise,
The general and the specific,
And put them earnestly into practice.

Consider the difference between the buddhas
Who accomplish the benefit for others
And we ordinary beings whose goal is our own
    benefit.
Even at the cost of your life, don't give up
    bodhichitta.

Since bodhichitta is the very root
Of the oceanlike activity of the bodhisattvas,
Know it to be the crux of all trainings,
The root of the Mahayana path.

If you have bodhichitta, you will go on the right
    path;
All that you do, even neutral actions,
Will turn into virtue,
And you will never stray from the path of total
    liberation.

Without bodhichitta, whatever you do
Will keep you on the lesser path;
Even your virtuous deeds will perpetuate samsara,
Not to speak of neutral and other deeds.
Whatever you do, it will all be suffering.

Therefore you must examine your mind again
    and again
With presence, awareness, and concern.
Never think that it is a small offense
To break the minor precepts.

Having asked the buddhas and bodhisattvas
To give you their attention,
You donned the armor of vowing to liberate all beings,
Thus gladdening gods and men.

So if you deceive them now,
What will become of all these sentient beings?

It has been said that through perseverance
Even bees and flies can achieve enlightenment.
Why should you, a human being,
Lack courage?

With familiarity,
Everything gets easier;
Repeating your efforts over and over,
You must train your mind.

Although I have not done it the slightest harm,
My enemy, ego-clinging,
Has entrenched itself in my heart since
    beginningless time
And confined me to the appalling prison of
    existence.

It has inflicted hundreds of tortures upon me.
Yet instead of resenting it,
I have put my trust in it and fallen under its
    power.
Is there any catastrophe, any delusion
Worse than this?

Misplaced patience is contemptible.
Taking the Three Jewels as my support,
Mounting the horse of irrevocable renunciation,
Donning the armor of the four boundless ones,
And rallying the armies of the six paramitas,
Today, with the sharp weapons of emptiness and
    compassion,
I shall slay my foe!

If I do not destroy ego-clinging,
It will continue to generate the endless torments
Of the hell Without Respite and others.
What sane being would fail to take action?

Examine where the nature of the "self"
Remains and goes to;
You will discover that it does not possess the
    slightest shred of existence.
It is an enemy that, once subdued,
Will never rise again.

In the past, the sublime, heroic bodhisattvas
Achieved bliss by conquering this very enemy.
Knowing the risks and benefits that are at stake,
One who does not let this enemy escape
Is the wisest of the wise,
The bravest of the brave.
Who can equal such a one?

The wise Victorious Ones
Expounded eighty-four thousand teachings
To subdue ego-clinging,
Tailored to the faculties of every being to be taught.

All are for the single purpose of taming
    self-clinging.
Depending on the level of one's intelligence,
The obscuring emotions can be eradicated,
    transformed, or utilized.
Yet in essence the root of all these
Is the supreme training: bodhichitta.

How is one to practice?
Not allowing free rein to ordinary thoughts

That fabricate samsara,
Master them with mindfulness.
Recollect all your past anger
And completely crush it with the army of the
    antidotes:
This is giving up the obscuring emotions.

Then to completely purify the entire field of
    your action,
Like turning iron into gold,
With relative bodhichitta, transform the three
    objects, the three poisons, and the three root merits.

Finally, practicing absolute bodhichitta,
Realize that whatever arises is the display of
    dharmakaya,
The primordial nature, unbroken simplicity.
Without clinging, whatever arises is naturally freed.
In the great equal taste without rejecting or
    accepting,
Continue on.

The meaning, the primordial indivisibility of
    wisdom and skillful means,
Emptiness with compassion as its very essence,
Must be carried onto the path.

However, to gradually gain steadiness of mind,
Beginners must first practice relative bodhichitta.
To do this, know that all sentient beings have been
    your mother,
Ponder their kindness and think of a way to repay it.

Develop gentle love and the rest of the four
    boundless qualities,
Especially the miraculous great compassion.

Meditating stage by stage upon the objects
Toward which these four arise very easily,
Relatively easily, and with difficulty,
Train yourself in these four immeasurables through
various methods.

Since one cannot make absolute judgments,
You and all beings are equal in wanting happiness;
You and all beings are equal in wanting to avoid
suffering.

In order to become used to caring for others more
than yourself,
You should bring to mind the essential points and
integrate in your being
The visualizations for exchanging self and others,
While riding the horse of the breath.

Do not count this practice,
Nor measure it in terms of days, months, or years.
Ask whether true experience has been born within
or not
And be sincere in making bodhichitta an
all-embracing,
Profound, integral part of yourself.

In order to weaken whatever contradicts this
practice
And to strengthen whatever assists it,
You should, to the utmost of your ability,
Purify your obscurations, perfect the accumulations,
And pray repeatedly to the guru and the Three Jewels,
Putting all your hopes in them.

When your own happiness increases
Or when you simply have desire for it,

You must understand that virtuous deeds lead to
  happiness.

Therefore at all times gather your energy
And generously dedicate it to all sentient beings,
Praying that your happiness and virtuous deeds
May nurture all beings.

When you see others acting virtuously,
Rejoice from your heart,
Without animosity or jealousy,
And pray that everyone may act likewise.

When undesirable things come to pass
Or when you simply wish to be rid of sufferings,
You must understand that these are proof
That their cause, nonvirtue, must be eliminated.
Mustering the four powers,
Attack the one responsible: ego-clinging.

Pray that all the degeneration and faults,
Which are the causes, conditions, and results
Of the suffering of an infinite number of beings,
May ripen upon you,
And that all beings may become free of their
  sufferings,
Which are but the result of their own negative
  actions.

Especially whenever any of the five poisonous
  emotions,
Or any of the eight worldly concerns arise,
Seize hold of them with fresh presence of mind.

As a mental exercise to vanquish ego-clinging,
Recollect all the times you have been wronged.

First think of all the obscuring emotions
And the notion that beings and phenomena truly
    exist,
Which create obstacles to the higher aspirations
Of all beings in general and of Dharma practitioners
    in particular,
And the difficulties and adversities arising from these.

Then gather all of them with your inhalation,
Dissolve it into your own ego-clinging,
And destroy the curse itself.
Gather into one essential point
A fierce determination to eliminate ego-clinging
Together with its antidote
And the meditation practice that averts it.

This is what propels the practice.
Though seemingly insignificant, it is the very crux
And brings the greatest progress on the path.
That is the relative mind training.

Since it is said,
"There is immeasurable virtue
In wanting to cure even the mildest headache of
    a single being.
What about wanting to dispel
All of the sufferings of all sentient beings?"

Once you grow familiar with this,
Develop absolute bodhichitta.
All discernible appearances, both outer and inner
    phenomena,
Are like dreams and illusions—
In the past they did not exist,
In the end they will not exist,

And in between they appear through a chain of
interdependent factors.

Although they appear,
From the very beginning phenomena are empty of
true existence;
Intrinsically, they are without essence,
Nor do they remain.
The expression is the kayas and wisdoms,
Yet the absolute nature never changes:
As it was, so it shall be.

Not knowing this, childish sentient beings
Treat phenomena as if they were solid and real.
Thus begins a chain of attractions and aversions
And the great sufferings of this existence—
a nonexistent masquerade!

The powerful roots are ignorance
And assuming that beings and phenomena truly
exist,
When these become habitual,
Conditioned existence arises.

Following the scriptures and the guru's pith
instructions,
Fortunate beings who aspire to freedom
Must first acquaint themselves
With the nonexistence of beings and phenomena.

Clinging to the notion that a self actually exists
Is taking the thought of "I" to be an actual entity
And results from a mistaken apprehension
Of the perishable five aggregates.

If one examines properly
The collection of these five aggregates,

Which are multiple and impermanent,
Like lightning, a waterfall, or a butter lamp,
One sees, as when mistaking a rope for a snake,
That the self is nothing but a misperception:
It is nonexistent, devoid of intrinsic reality.

Clinging to the notion that phenomena truly exist
Is clinging to the notion of subject and object.
All the objects one apprehends, outer and inner
     phenomena,
Are illusory appearances resulting from habitual
     tendencies.

Like visual aberrations,
Like reflections of the moon on water, and like
     mistaken perceptions,
When unexamined they are taken for granted;
When examined they are seen to be nothing at all.

Phenomena are not definable entities
As atoms and seconds would be.
Therefore you must conclude that subject and object
Cannot in any way be said to exist.

By continuously turning the wheel of investigation,
You will gain confidence
In the nonexistence of both beings and phenomena
And a time will come when you achieve certainty
That the two truths,
The illusory arising of interdependent events
And the emptiness that is devoid of all assumptions,
Are not contradictory but, in essence, one.

When all preconceptions that assert separation
Between manifestation and emptiness collapse,
Investigation comes to an end.
Then what is the use of conceptual reasoning?

Emptiness is the antidote to all views,
But if one clings to the concept of emptiness,
Like a purgative turned into poison,
It becomes ineffective.

Like two sticks that when rubbed together
Are consumed in the fire of their own making,
The antidote itself must disappear of its own accord.

Relax in the continuum of primordial simplicity,
Which is the absolute nature that remains since the
    beginning,
The natural state, the expanse endowed with the
    three doors of liberation:
Emptiness, absence of characteristics, and absence of
    intent.

Then you will see the radiant buddha-nature,
In which all fabrications and workings of mind
Are at peace in the absolute expanse.

Empty by nature, it is free from eternalism;
Cognizant in its expression, it is free from nihilism.
Although one thus considers two aspects,
It is the basic nature in which
All notions of dualistic perception are freed in their
    own space:
Inconceivable, ineffable, apprehended by wisdom
    alone,

Uncompounded by nature,
Seen without seeing,
As when gazing into vajra space,
It is called "seeing the sky of the absolute."

There is nothing to dispel
Nor the slightest thing to add.

Looking perfectly at perfection itself,
Seeing perfection, one is perfectly liberated.

When tangible things and intangible things
Cease to remain present in the mind,
In the absence of other alternatives,
Naked of all concepts, this is complete peace.

Unaware of this vital point,
To painfully nail down your mind
With mental fabrications is not calm-abiding;
To construct intellectual boundaries is not insight.

To see perfectly the inconceivable absolute nature,
Without any intellectual fabrications,
Is an example of pristine wisdom.

Beyond this, the supreme absolute wisdom—
The field of understanding of the sublime beings
Who have reached the state of unity,
The meaning of the primordial union of insight—
That brings about the wisdom and tranquillity of
Remaining in the continuum of the natural state,
Will be realized by the power of the guru's pith
    instructions.

Meditation experiences tainted by the notion of true
    existence,
Whether bliss, clarity, or nonthought,
Are all deceptive and misleading.
If you cling to things as real, you feed samsara
And will never transcend the three worlds.

Therefore, with consummate skill,
Rest in simplicity, letting everything be
In a state free of taking things as real,

In which the one who realizes, the realized, and
  realization
Become inseparable, like pouring water into water.

This is the fundamental nature beyond speech and
  intellect,
The definitive meaning, the transcendent perfection
  of wisdom
That can only be realized through one's own
  awareness.
Be determined to master this understanding!

In brief, as the protector Atisha said,
"Within the absolute, there are no distinctions;
There are neither conditioned phenomena nor
  absolute phenomena.
In the face of emptiness, there are no distinctions,
  none at all.

"Realizing this without realization
Is called simply 'seeing emptiness,'
Seeing what cannot be seen.
So it is said in the most profound sutras.
Nothing to see, no one who sees,
No beginning, no end,
Peace.

"Utterly beyond 'really there' and 'not really there,'
Free of classification and reference point,
It does not cease, does not remain,
Never comes, never goes.
It cannot be captured in words.

"It cannot be expressed; it cannot be viewed;
It never changes and has never ever existed as a solid
  reality.

The yogi who realizes this
Rids himself of the two veils: the veil of the
    obscuring emotions
And the veil covering all that is to be known."
So said Atisha in *Entering the Two Truths*.

The eight qualities of understanding the ultimate
    truth
Are expounded in the sutras, and
All this falls naturally into place in the Great
    Perfection
By pointing out the true nature of mind,
Which is achieved through direct transmission
Effected by the guru's blessings.
This is not within the scope of ordinary minds,
And those who are experts at discursive thought
Will have no taste of it.
"Absolute truth, arisen from itself,
Is realized through faith alone."
So it is said.

Therefore hold on to the vital force of devotion
That sees the guru as dharmakaya.
Relax into unbroken pristine simplicity,
And you will realize the essential meaning.

If you miss this vital point
And complacently believe that you have not strayed
    into heretical deviations,
Or claim that you make no assertions
Or cling to emptiness as a bare nothingness,
That is not the Middle Way.

If you fail to destroy the mental fixations
Of a materialistic point of view,
You have strayed even further from the Middle Way.

Therefore foster freedom from clinging and all
    mental constructs.

So-called great meditators who fail to realize this,
Afraid that their practice will starve itself to death,
Are zealously torturing themselves.
What's the point of that?
What's the point of keeping track
Of the comings and goings of thoughts?

"Wakeful awareness that is beyond the
    consciousnesses,"
"Dharmakaya beyond the fundamental
    consciousness,"
"Freedom from the conditioned intellect,"
I am sorry to say that none of these
Are actually heard by ordinary beings
And the meaning remains untapped,
But I won't say too much about it.

All beings have tathagatagarbha
And thus they all possess the cause for buddhahood.
So view all of them as pure
And consider their great kindness.

Between practice sessions,
Develop generosity and the other paramitas,
Without the three concepts.
Dedicate everything toward great enlightenment.
Such is the excellent path uniting the two
    accumulations.

Thus the path of bodhichitta
In which both relative and absolute truths are one—
Emptiness with the essence of compassion—
Is the path that gladdens the Victorious Ones.

Meditate upon it continually and before long,
As the veils masking buddha-nature are cleared
away,
You will earn the title of "enlightened one."

Having actualized stainless, excellent qualities,
Manifesting ceaseless, omnipresent, and
spontaneous buddha activity,
You will act as a protector of all beings under
the skies.

*Thus I, Padma Vijaya, having drunk the instructions
that streamed forth from the mouths of the great lineage
holders, have looked a little into them and now, having
a little experience of them, at the request of a noble
Dharma friend, I have spoken this short explanation.*

By this merit may the altruistic awakened mind
Be born in the mind streams of all sentient beings.
May they see the ultimate truth unveiled,
The very face of buddha-nature.

Translated by Matthieu Ricard at Shechen Monastery in
Kham, Tibet, July 9, 1988.

PART ONE

VIRTUOUS
AT THE
BEGINNING

I

INTRODUCTION
TO THE TEXT

The root text in Tibetan can be found in Volume 5 (CA) of the *Collected Works of Shechen Gyaltsap Pema Namgyal* published by Lama Ngodup in Paro, Bhutan, 1975–1994. (The collected works of *ze-chen rgyal-tshab padma-rnam-rgyal / ze chen rgyal tshab kyi bka' 'bum.*) A new more complete edition is being prepared by Shechen Publications and will be available by 2008.

THE AUTHOR

Shechen Gyaltsap Gyurme Pema Namgyal, a remarkable master who lived at the end of the nineteenth and the beginning of the twentieth century, wrote *The Great Medicine That Conquers Clinging to the Notion of Reality.* He was a disciple of the greatest luminaries of the nineteenth century, including Jamyang Khyentse Wangpo, Jamgon Kongtrol Lodro Thaye, and Lama Mipham Rinpoche. Shechen Gyaltsap was indisputably one of the most learned and accomplished lamas of his time. The thirteen volumes of his writings contain many lucid and profound commentaries on various aspects of philosophy and practice.

Shechen Gyaltsap was also an accomplished practitioner. He spent much of his life in retreat above Shechen Monastery in eastern Tibet and achieved many signs of accomplishment. Once he started a three-year retreat based on the *Vajrakilaya* practice, but to everyone's surprise he emerged after only three months, saying that he had completed his intended program. The next morning, his attendant noticed an imprint of the sole of his foot on the stone threshold of the hermitage, an outer sign of his inner realization of the Vajrakilaya practice. During the Cultural Revolution, Shechen Gyaltsap's disciples removed the stone and hid it, but it is possible to see it today at Shechen Monastery.

Shechen Gyaltsap provided the first root teachings to both Dilgo Khyentse Rinpoche—whom he recognized as an emanation of Jamyang Khyentse Wangpo—and Dzongzar Khyentse Chokyi Lodro at his hermitage. In his autobiography Khyentse Rinpoche wrote about his teacher:

> While he was giving empowerments, I was often overwhelmed by the splendor and magnificence of his expression and his eyes as, with a gesture pointing in my direction, he introduced the nature of mind. I felt that, apart from my own feeble devotion causing me to see him as an ordinary man, he was in fact exactly the same as the great Guru Padmasambhava giving empowerments to the twenty-five disciples. My confidence grew stronger and stronger, and when again he would gaze and point at me, asking "What is the nature of mind?" I would think with great devotion, "This is truly a great yogi who can see the absolute nature of reality!" and I myself began to understand how to meditate.[4]

THE TEXT

Like many traditional texts, this one has three parts: the virtuous beginning, the virtuous middle, and the virtuous end. The virtuous beginning is the introduction, the virtuous middle is the main teaching itself, and the virtuous end is the colophon and dedication. The introduction has four parts: the title, the homage paid by the author, the statement of the author's intention in writing the text, and the need for such a teaching.

The Title

The full title of the teaching is *The Great Medicine That Conquers Clinging to the Notion of Reality: Steps in Meditation on the Enlightened Mind.* Depending on the reader's knowledge, realization, and intellectual capacity, the title of a book serves various functions. A knowledgeable practitioner of the highest intelligence and understanding will know exactly what the book is about just by hearing its title. This type of practitioner is rather like a skillful doctor who reads a medicine label and knows immediately when and how to use it. Someone of average intelligence will understand to which aspects of the Buddhist teachings it pertains—in this case, the teachings of Mahayana. Finally, for those of us with lesser faculties, the title simply makes it easier for us to find the book.

The Homage

> Namo Guru Buddha Bodhisattva
> Homage to the gurus, buddhas, and bodhisattvas!

The homage is written in both Sanskrit and Tibetan, both of which translate as "Homage to the gurus, buddhas, and bodhisattvas!"

The author includes the Sanskrit homage to remind the reader that most of the canonical teachings were translated from

Sanskrit and that the fundamental teachings of Buddhism, which originated in India, are the basis for this text. The homage also carries the blessing of the Buddha's lineage and creates a propensity to learn the original language of the Buddha's teachings.

> I bow to all the masters
> Who have attained supreme primordial liberation
> And out of compassion remain here,
> Dredging the depths of samsara.

The extended homage follows the Sanskrit homage. It is usually paid to whomever is most closely related to the teachings or is its source, whether this is a a buddha, bodhisattva, or spiritual teacher. The meaning of "spiritual teacher" varies, depending on the depth of your practice and the purity of your vision. The Hinayana path of individual liberation sees the teacher simply as a spiritual friend; the Mahayana considers the teacher as a bodhisattva; and the Vajrayana, or "Secret Mantra," perceives the teacher as the Buddha.

Since this text deals with the Vajrayana, we pay homage to the teacher as being one with the Buddha himself. When we use the word *Buddha,* we are not referring only to the historical figure Gautama Buddha, who began with an ordinary human existence and then gradually attained buddhahood in that particular lifetime. Instead we view the Buddha from the Vajrayana perspective, as one who has already attained buddhahood and recognized the primordial perfection, the ultimate nature of things. He manifests in our world in order to show sentient beings the path of the accumulation of merit and wisdom that ultimately leads to the achievement of buddhahood. His compassion for all sentient beings is the only reason the Buddha manifested as a spiritual teacher in an ordinary samsaric existence, intent upon "dredging the depths of samsara" and freeing all sentient beings from suffering.

The Author's Intention

The next verse is a declaration of the author's purpose for writing this text and includes an introduction to the subject. He announces his teaching by saying,

> I will speak a little about how to destroy one's
>   clinging to the notion of reality
> With the great medicine, bodhichitta,
> The essence of the Mahayana path,
> The road traveled by all the buddhas and
>   bodhisattvas.

Bodhichitta, the altruistic wish to attain enlightenment for the sake of all sentient beings, is the indispensable life force of the Mahayana path to enlightenment. Chandrakirti's *Entry into the Middle Way* states, "The arhats and listeners, the shravakas, and pratyekabuddhas, all achieved their respective levels by listening to the Buddha's teachings and putting them into practice."[5] But the Buddha himself achieved enlightenment chiefly through bodhichitta and compassion, the very roots of buddhahood.

All buddhas and bodhisattvas, without exception, achieved enlightenment through the practice of bodhichitta—the great medicine that heals us. Our sickness is the idea of self and other, the notion of a personal identity, and the belief in the reality of phenomena. This clinging is the cause of all suffering and the main obstacle to achieving enlightenment. The medicine of compassion and an altruistic mind that aspires to free all beings from suffering is the cure.

The Need for the Teachings

The last section of the introduction explains why there is a need for this teaching.

> Keep this in mind when in dire straits
> Upon the vast plain of clinging to life's appearances,

Surrounded by your enemies—the obscuring
emotions—
You are about to be robbed of the supreme wealth—
virtue.

Travelers on the journey of existence live with the constant threat of bandits and enemies. Who are these robbers? They are our own afflictive emotions and negative states; they rob us of the precious treasures we carry on our journey. They take all the positive aspects of mind that allow us to travel the path to enlightenment.

In many parts of ancient Tibet, bandits on horseback would wait to rob travelers. Nowadays, throughout the world, there is another type of bandit that tries to rob our minds. I was recently in Times Square. Every second in every direction, bright, flashing advertisements tried to steal my mind and direct it toward grasping, wanting things, craving, and clinging. This clinging creates a vast plain of deluded existence, where we cling to whatever appears and take for granted that things actually exist as they appear. These thieves—obscuring emotions—do not need to ride a horse to catch their victims.

We are constantly caught in the mechanism of repulsion and aversion—trying to hold on to our possessions, our relatives, and whatever else we consider ours. We stay caught in a constant pattern of delusion as we try to destroy our enemies or discard what seems to be threatening to the self. Clinging to this life's appearances, we are bound by the eight worldly preoccupations of gain and loss, fame and obscurity, pain and pleasure, and praise and blame. These hopes and fears will rob us of the jewel of bodhichitta.

How can we defeat these bandits?

PART TWO

VIRTUOUS IN THE MIDDLE

The Main Teaching

2

IDENTIFYING THE
AWAKENED MIND

The main teaching is also divided into three parts. The first part describes bodhichitta, the enlightened mind; the second part explains how to train in bodhichitta; and the third part discusses the results of practicing bodhichitta.

The verses describe bodhichitta from the perspective of absolute truth. They then investigate how our recognition of absolute truth is lost through delusion and how we become deluded. Lastly, they explain how to dispel delusion in order to rediscover our true nature.

How the Awakened Mind Is Present in Everyone

The following two verses describe the nature of absolute truth and its presence in all sentient beings.

> All phenomena remain in the expanse
> Of beginningless time;

Since this is the case,
All sentient beings can achieve nirvana.

Just as there is perfectly clear water
Within the earth,
Within the obscuring emotions,
There is great primordial wisdom.

As it says in the scriptures, "All sentient beings without exception have buddha-nature." "Great primordial wisdom" (*tathagatagarbha*) is the absolute bodhichitta, or buddha-nature, that is present in all sentient beings. Yet this wisdom is obscured by a transient veil of delusion.

How does this obscured or deluded state affect buddhanature? "Just as there is perfectly clear water within the earth." Although it may not be realized, primordial wisdom dwells within the obscuring emotions that invade and condition the mind. Just as the pure water that flows underground cannot be seen on the surface, within the realm of obscuring emotions and confusion, the great primordial wisdom remains unchanged.

Sometimes you might doubt that all sentient beings have buddha-nature. You might find it hard to imagine that this potential for compassion exists in everyone when violence, massacres, genocide, and ethnic cleansing are happening throughout the world. You might even begin to believe that human nature is basically evil. But this is not the case. If, through introspection and meditation, you look deeply at the mind itself, you will apprehend the most fundamental aspect of consciousness—pure awareness. This basic nature of the mind remains unspoiled even though obscuring emotions might temporarily cover it.

The sutras that elucidate emptiness,
And all the words spoken by the Victorious Ones,
Speak of getting rid of the obscuring emotions.

There are three main categories of Buddhist teachings known as the *Tripitaka*. They explain the emptiness of the intrinsic existence of all phenomena. They help to clear away obscuring emotions and toxic mental factors such as hatred, desire, mental confusion, pride, and jealousy. By nature these afflictive emotions are ephemeral states that are not intrinsically present in the primordial nature of mind. Therefore, although these emotions might seem to poison the mind, the basic buddha-nature always remains immaculate and unstained. We need to dispel the veils that obscure buddha-nature. The text discusses how we can accomplish this.

> Buddha-nature is immaculate.
> It is profound, serene, unfabricated suchness,
> An uncompounded expanse of luminosity;
> Nonarising, unceasing, primordial peace,
> Spontaneously present nirvana.

Buddha-nature is the luminous, ceaseless, and primordial nature of mind. "Uncompounded" means that it has not been fabricated or created by various causes and conditions. It does not dwell as a separate entity that truly exists. It did not begin, and therefore it cannot cease. It is simply the ultimate nature of phenomena:

> Just as sesame oil pervades sesame seeds,
> The essence of the tathagatas
> Is primordially present and inseparable from
> The basic state of all beings.

Just as oil saturates sesame seeds, buddha-nature pervades sentient beings. It is "the basic state of all beings," meaning the absolute or true nature of mind, the *dharmata*. Buddha-nature dwells in all of us because it is the ultimate nature of mind. It is not something that is fabricated. It has always been with us and it is not separate from us.

How Delusion Arises

All sentient beings have buddha-nature; however, we easily lose sight of it:

> Obscured by the deluded notions of subject and
> object,
> Shrouded in the cocoon of the three habitual
> tendencies,
> Like a treasure lying hidden in a poor man's house,
> This nature remains unrecognized.

In our deluded state, we are like a man who, unaware of the treasure buried under his house, believes he is poor when he is actually quite rich. Likewise, the treasure of buddha-nature is buried within us. We live as paupers without awareness or recognition of our own inherent wealth. We fall into delusion when we forget our buddha-nature and see the world in terms of self and other.

Delusion occurs when we reify the phenomenal world and ourselves. This notion of being separate is just a mental fabrication, since neither self nor other truly exists. It is our notion of subject and object that creates a chain of dualistic, habitual tendencies related to the external world, our mind, and our body.

Let's analyze in more detail how these "deluded notions of subject and object" come about. There are three types of habitual tendencies that make delusions thicker, until they completely enshroud us in a cocoon of ignorance.

The first relates to the beings and objects we perceive to be the external world—all that we feel is "out there" or whatever we perceive through the five senses. We attribute values to what we see, imagining it to be intrinsically pleasurable, unpleasant, or neutral. Then we follow the process of wanting anything pleasurable, repelling that which is unpleasant, and neglecting what seems to be neutral. In doing so, we weave a cocoon of delusion and suffering like a caterpillar imprisoning itself inside a shell of its own making.

The second habitual tendency relates to consciousness, the inner subject that grasps at external "things." The inner subject functions with the eight aspects of consciousness. The first and underlying consciousness, the *alaya-vijnana*, is merely being aware of the world. Various other aspects of consciousness that relate to the five senses of sight, sound, taste, smell, and touch follow. Then comes an aspect of consciousness related to the *kleshas*, the different mental poisons. These taint and obscure the intellect, which is the eighth aspect. Thus the activity of the eight aspects of consciousness creates the notion of a separate "inner" subject.

The third habitual tendency comes from our perception of the body. In Tibetan, the word for body is *lu*, which literally means "something that is left behind." *Lu* refers to the fact that we abandon the body when we die, after which it disintegrates. Consequently, *lu* denotes the body's ephemeral and composite nature. Nevertheless, we create a very strong habitual tendency by clinging to the idea of our own body and the notion that we have all of our experiences through the body. In fact, we tend to associate all experiences of suffering and pleasure with the notion of a body. Even in dreams, we believe our body experiences sensations such as being burned, falling into water, or going through different trials and tribulations.

These three types of habitual tendencies accumulate on the ground of the basic consciousness and become ever stronger. This is what creates our mental disposition of confusion and ignorance.

> Obscuring emotions and wrong actions
> Cause sufferings to fall upon us like rain.

Since beginningless time you have roamed
On the immense plain of existence, which is
    apparent yet unreal.
Alas! Such is the power of ignorance and karma.

The obscuring emotions and the mistaken actions they engender "cause sufferings to fall upon us like rain." Suffering is a result of actions of body, speech, and mind. These actions are triggered or motivated by obscuring emotions that continue to generate one after another, continuously creating more suffering. This cycle has been going on since beginningless time, and thus we wander without direction in the conditioned existence of samsara.

However, samsara is not what it seems to be. "Which is apparent yet unreal" indicates that although this plain of existence seems real and solid, its ultimate nature is also devoid of any intrinsic existence. Upon examination, we can find that it is unreal.

How to Be Free of Delusion

Having fully prostrated
At the lotus feet of an authentic master,
You should cleanse the stains of ego-clinging
With the nectar of his instructions.

To dispel the confusion, we need to find an authentic spiritual teacher. We need to be skillful in finding such a teacher, skillful in practicing the teachings, and finally, skillful in putting them into action. Many instructions in the scriptures enumerate the qualities of an authentic teacher. The text *The Words of My Perfect Teacher*[6] devotes a whole chapter to this subject. We should know these important qualities before committing ourselves.

The teacher's qualities are important because we need a spiritual master to help us free ourselves from afflictive emotions. To be wholly concerned with benefiting beings, the teacher must also be free of such emotions and worldly preoccupations. After finding a fully qualified teacher, we should strive to eliminate our obscurations as if we were removing stains from a cloth. Only the nectar of the teacher's oral instructions can help us to remove the "stain" of clinging to the notions of self and phenomena.

Once we are committed to the path, we need to know how and where to begin. The path itself has various stages. First, we need to establish the foundation with the preliminaries of the four reflections. Then we make the aspiration to seek refuge. In the third and main part, we generate enlightened mind, or bodhichitta.

3

PRELIMINARIES AND REFUGE

The four reflections that turn the mind away from samsara and toward the Dharma are called *preliminaries*. This term might create the false impression that they are not of primary importance, but this is not the case. In fact, the preliminaries are the foundation on which all practice is built. Although they are called preliminaries, we should think of them as the main practice. If we engage in these four preliminaries—reflecting upon the value of human existence, death and impermanence, the shortcomings of samsara, and the law of causality—there is no doubt that we will develop a genuine wish to escape samsara and eagerly pursue the path. This wish, called renunciation, is what impels us to stay on the path, take refuge, and so forth.

Many of us have often heard about these four mind changes. We might say, "Let's just get right to the pith instructions and not waste time." But the life stories of the great practitioners in Tibet show how much they valued and immersed themselves in these preliminaries.

Masters of the past reflected on the truth of impermanence and the preciousness of human existence for months, if not years. They did not think, "It's great to have this human existence; it's quite valuable. Let's move on to other practices." Rather, they developed a direct and stable recognition of the true value of human existence and a constant awareness of impermanence. As a result of this appreciation, their urge to practice became second nature. Jamyang Khyentse Wangpo wrote that he achieved the most profound spiritual realization by genuinely experiencing the four changes of attitude.

Once Patrul Rinpoche went to meet a great meditator in retreat. Patrul Rinpoche was a very realized and learned person, yet he asked this hermit for teachings on these four reflections that many people consider to be very basic. The hermit was not surprised. On the first day, he uttered a sentence about the rarity and preciousness of human existence: "Alas! Freedom and favorable conditions are so difficult to obtain." Then he just sat quietly. The two great masters began to weep, overwhelmed by the truth of this statement, and they sat silently for the rest of the session. The next day, the hermit said, "Life rushes by like a mountain cascade." Having contemplated this line, they again began to shed tears. And so it continued with only one sentence being spoken on each of four days. Later, Patrul Rinpoche said that these were the most profound teachings he ever received because they were so experiential. They transformed him from within. A teacher might ask you to practice each of the reflections for a month so that the teachings really become a part of you.

Precious Human Birth

> Now that you have at last obtained
> This free, privileged human birth,
> Which is so hard to find and so meaningful,
> It is worthwhile to transform your being in solitude
> Without being attached to this life,
> Which is of such small importance.

According to the Buddhist teachings, there are many other realms or states of being. None of them, however, are as conducive to engaging on the path of Dharma as is human birth. For example, celestial beings are gods with incredibly long lives. In their celestial realms, everything seems to be easy and all their needs, including every comfort and pleasure, are fulfilled. However, all this comfort and happiness easily distract them. Beings in this state of existence lack the incentive to become interested in Dharma practice. Finally, at the time of death, they foresee how they are powerlessly going to lose their god-life and fall back into the suffering of the lower realms, and they experience the most horrendous suffering.

Human existence is unique in having just enough suffering to make us want to be free of suffering, yet not so much that we cannot practice. To maximize this precious opportunity, it is "worthwhile to transform your being in solitude." It seems pointless to have a human existence and not take full advantage of it. People tend to waste this potential through indifference or, even worse, by engaging in destructive and negative actions. Our lives will be a mere imitation of how truly meaningful the human experience can be if we do not cherish this precious opportunity.

A Tibetan teacher once said that, compared to all other possible existences, to be born as a human being is as rare as the specks of dust on one fingernail compared to all the dust on earth. Missing the point, a student from China said, "If the Tibetans came to China, they would see that human existence is not rare at all. China is full of people." It may be that the earth is becoming overpopulated, but there are still far fewer humans than there are members of other species, and among the human beings who do exist, very few live a truly meaningful life. Ask yourself how many people realize the preciousness of this life. Of those, how many think of using it to practice the Dharma? How many of them actually start to practice? Of those who start, how many continue?

Since it is so hard to find, yet so meaningful to have, why does Shechen Gyaltsap write that this life "is of such small importance"? The reason is twofold. First, our ordinary preoccupations and mundane pursuits are not really very important and distract us from the path that can bring immense benefits for many lifetimes to come. Second, this life is just one brief episode among many past and future lives. We need a much wider perspective than the one that is entangled in petty concerns or the temporary success of the moment. Once we begin to concentrate on our spiritual practice, we soon discover that it is the best use of our time. Peace and solitude are conducive to concentration and give rise to fewer distractions. Such conditions help beginners develop, stabilize, and deepen their meditation practice.

When we hear about renouncing samsara, we might feel scared and think, "Samsara is so familiar and engaging, why should I abandon it?" We fear that this means we must give up wonderful things, and it is absurd to give up something pleasant. However, in this case, we are not giving up anything that is authentically good, but rather freeing ourselves from trouble. A true analogy for renunciation is the act of freeing a bird from a golden cage. It would be odd if the bird thought that the cage was nicer than the sky and did not seek its freedom.

Sometimes samsara and its pleasures seem very appealing. It is a little bit like traveling in India when, after a long bus journey on busy roads, you come to a small roadside restaurant. Chapatis and curries are displayed beautifully, ready to be eaten. You can smell the delicious spices. Just to see the dishes makes you salivate, and you want to sit down and eat right away. But then you go around to the back and have a look at the kitchen. One cook with a big belly is sweating profusely over the food, while another cook is kneading dough with his feet. The uncooked food looks spoiled and there are flies and smoke everywhere. When you go back and look at your plate, you feel disgusted and not as eager to eat as before.

Likewise, samsara appears to be attractive at first. But if you look at it in the same way you did the food and the kitchen, you notice that the afflictive emotions are busy preparing all the samsaric pleasures you crave: the chocolate cake of desire, the chilies of anger, and the sweet-and-sour sauce of jealousy. You immediately lose your appetite for what at first glance looked so mouthwatering. Once you realize the truth, you will find it much easier to leave your craving behind, and renunciation becomes easy and natural.

Even if we recognize the true value of human existence, we can still fall prey to inertia and laziness. Laziness is the main obstacle to making the most of this life and putting the Dharma into practice. We always postpone practice, saying, "Oh, I'll do that later, when I have some free time or when I retire." But with this attitude, the time will never come. The sutras repeatedly emphasize meditation on thoughts of impermanence and death as a way to dispel laziness. These thoughts spur us on to practice. That is why Shechen Gyaltsap wrote,

> Amid the clouds of impermanence and illusion
> The lightning of life dances:
> Are you sure you won't die tomorrow?
> Death is unavoidable, so practice the Dharma!

IMPERMANENCE

When we go on vacation, we make elaborate preparations; we book flights, make hotel reservations, plan what to take, and so on. If we are going hiking or skiing, we begin to exercise to get in shape. We put a lot of time and energy into just one vacation. Yet we are apathetic about preparing for our own death. Why are we are so casual about the most momentous trip that awaits us? We are going to leave this body, but we are not interested in preparing ourselves for the inevitable journey on which only our karma will accompany us like a shadow. Our differing attitudes toward these two types of trips seem disproportionate when we compare their relative importance.

We are not always aware of impermanence, although we are surrounded by it on many different levels. Gross and subtle levels of impermanence exist everywhere in the external universe. Today, near Bodhgaya, shabby huts made of tin and plastic sheets cover a small hill that, in the time of the Buddha, hosted a vast monastic congregation with a great number of communities studying and practicing. Barely a stone of that monastery is left; memories are all that remain.

People are also impermanent. In fact, everyone is subject to impermanence; it does not discriminate between enlightened beings and ordinary beings. We all age, get sick, and die; no one can escape this cycle. The conditions of our own lives are constantly changing. We might be rich one day and bankrupt the next, or vice versa. However much we wish the opposite, there is nothing lasting or permanent that we can rely on.

Yet we grasp at things hoping to find happiness. Normally we do not even bother to try to hold on to something that we know can last for only a fraction of a second. This is why reflecting on the transitory nature of human existence lessens our attraction to and rejection of the things of this world. The more we meditate on impermanence, the more our grasping and, hence, our impulses of attachment and repulsion diminish.

All the great practitioners of the past took impermanence as one of their main subjects of reflection. The great meditator Kharak Gomchung stayed in a cave with a thorny bush at the entrance. Each time he exited the cave, his robes would get caught on the thorns, and he would say, "I should cut that thorn bush down." But then, moments later, he would change his mind and think, "Oh, what's the use? Who knows if I will ever go back inside again or if I will still be alive even a few minutes from now?" Later, when entering the cave again, the same thing would happen, and he would think, "I should cut that bush, but who knows if I'll ever come out again? Better to make use of every minute and meditate rather than waste time." Kharak Gomchung had taken impermanence to heart, and after many years of retreat, that bush was still there as a reminder.

SHORTCOMINGS OF SAMSARA

The third reflection that changes our attitude is on the shortcomings of samara. As long as ignorance prevails, our conditioned existence will be nothing more than a veiled expression of suffering. This is why the very first teaching of the Buddha begins with "O Bhikshus, you should recognize the truth of suffering."

> Since beginningless time
> In the prison of existence,
> You have endured the punishment of the threefold
>   suffering.

There are obvious common sufferings such as pain, heat, cold, and so on. These sufferings come in succession and pile up on top of one another. That is the common experience of suffering. There is also a more subtle form. Usually we misapprehend what true happiness is; we fail to realize that what we now consider to be happiness is, in fact, permeated with suffering.

Even though our conventional sense of happiness seems to be at least momentarily enjoyable, it is bound to change into suffering. Its very nature is to become its opposite. For example, when we are in a cold house, we have the desire to get warm, so we go outside into the sunshine. At first the warmth of the sun is pleasant, and our shivering stops. But the longer we stay in the sun, the hotter we get, and this neutralizes our perception of pleasure.

Finally, we feel too hot; the sensation is too intense and becomes uncomfortable. Our initial happiness changes. The warmth that seemed pleasing at first no longer makes us happy and finally changes into a cause of suffering.

There is an even more subtle, all-pervading, and latent form of suffering. It concerns our propensity for clinging to the mistaken notion of a permanent self or ego and to the solid identity of phenomena. This grasping leads us to perceive phenomena as separate entities endowed with intrinsic qualities like beauty, ugliness, and so forth. Consequently, impulses of attraction and repulsion arise and create mental toxins that cause suffering and frustration. In this sense, ignorance, or the failure to recognize that phenomena simply arise as interdependent transitory events, is the fundamental cause of suffering. As long as ignorance is present, suffering will never be far away. Suffering is the nature of conditioned existence, but we do not recognize it. That is why the text states,

> Yet you remain unconcerned—rotten heart!
> Now is the time to conquer the citadel of great bliss.

"The citadel of great bliss" refers to enlightenment, the elimination of ignorance, and therefore the elimination of suffering. Rather than being a temporary relief, "great bliss" eradicates the cause of suffering itself.

THE LAW OF CAUSALITY

The fourth reflection is on the law of causality and addresses the question "How do happiness and suffering come about?" The Buddha taught that everything is the result of causes and conditions. This is the law of karma. The law of cause and effect is inescapable. It determines the shape not only of our present life, but also, according to Buddhist tradition, of our future, including the experience of various states of existence in lives to come.

Buddhists do not consider death an ending. The end of life is not like the moment when a flame goes out or a drop of water evaporates on a hot surface. Rather, Buddhists believe that consciousness continues, carrying with it the potential derived from all those activities and actions known as karma. Positive and negative actions determine the course of karma. Thus, recognizing and discriminating between positive actions that will bring happiness and negative actions that will result in suffering is of tremendous importance.

> Happiness and suffering are manifestations of
> karma.
> You cannot escape the law of cause and effect,
> So the Victorious One has said.
> Knowing this, discriminate carefully:
> Avoid evil deeds; accomplish virtuous acts.

Consider the following saying: "If you want to see what you were in the past, look at your body. If you want to see what you will be in the future, look at your actions." You did not come out of nowhere without cause. Neither predetermined destiny nor a divine creator imposed the circumstances of your life on you. What you are today is simply the result of a long chain of causes and effects. You can see from your own experience how past mistakes have serious consequences.

If you want to know your future, be mindful and reflect on what you are doing, thinking, and saying now. If you wish to avoid suffering and gain happiness, gather the causes and conditions that will bring about your well-being. Be mindful and check if your present actions, thoughts, and speech will be the cause for suffering or the source of happiness. Actions, thoughts, and speech do not necessarily bring about immediate results. They are more like seeds that have the potential to become flowers, trees, or fruit. Our past karma contains many latent seeds that have yet to blossom.

Consider this story. One of the Buddha's followers wanted to become a monk (*bhikshu*). Shariputra, the Buddha's disciple, used his power to summon up the past to try to find the seed that created this novice's wish. Among all the seeds in his past, there was one that seemed insignificant but was actually of great importance. This man had once been born as a pig that had been chased around a stupa by a dog. Although the man didn't know it, the pig had done a number of circumambulations around the holy monument. That seemingly small connection acted as the seed that eventually led him to follow a spiritual path.

Our past actions and mental imprints are infinitely complex. Where we are right now is no accident. Our current experience is the expression of many causes and conditions that have interwoven and are now coming to fruition.

The realization of emptiness brings about an even deeper understanding of the law of karma and a greater discernment in our actions. By realizing that phenomena are empty of autonomous existence, we understand that they can only arise because of dependence on each other. This understanding of interdependence reveals that a vast number of causes and conditions influence all of our actions. In order to experience happiness and avoid suffering, we need to examine our actions and thoughts and develop a subtle understanding of the law of causality. Highly realized practitioners do not neglect the law of cause and effect. In fact, their understanding leads them to use especially fine judgment and care in all they do and say.

The Root of the Path: Refuge in the Three Jewels

Contemplating the four reflections in depth will bring about a profound change in your attitude. You will realize how precious and fragile human existence actually is. By gaining confidence in the law of cause and effect and understanding that suffering pervades samsaric existence, you will naturally develop the desire to escape this vicious cycle. You will need someone to guide and help you find freedom—and not just anyone. You need someone endowed with the qualities of enlightenment.

> Rely upon the undeceiving embodiment of all
> refuges:
> The unexcelled Three Jewels.
> Just hearing their names
> Shatters the city of existence.

The Three Jewels are the Buddha, the Dharma, and the Sangha. The Buddha is the guide, the Dharma is the path, and the Sangha are our companions along the path.

What is meant by Buddha, or Sangye? *Sang* means "to have purified"; *gye* means "to have blossomed or increased." The Buddha is the one who discarded the two veils of emotional and cognitive obscurations[7] and developed the two wisdoms.[8]

The Dharma is what protects us against the different sufferings of samsara and the veils of mental confusion. It does this through two aspects: the transmission of the teachings (*tripitaka*) and the Dharma of realization (or what is achieved through the practice).

The Sangha is the community that has the qualities of freedom and liberation. Companions on a long journey are always valuable. The Sangha is especially precious because it accompanies us on the path. The members of the Sangha are "unexcelled" because they are free of ignorance and have the realization of the ultimate wisdom. Thus, they are worthy companions from whom we can seek assistance with complete trust. We are able to eradicate the root of ignorance and dispel the very cause of suffering by relying on them.

Taking refuge is like going through a door and finding ourselves on the Buddhist path. It is also like planting a seed that will eventually become a tree and bear fruit, given the right causes and conditions. The tree itself is the freedom from samsara, and the fruit is the recognition of the true nature of mind and the realization of the buddha-nature within all of us.

4

DEVELOPING THE AWAKENED MIND

In order to practice the Dharma, especially the Mahayana, we must change our self-centered attitude and become intimately concerned with the well-being of others. Up to this point, we have been concerned only with our own situation and learning how to free ourselves from samsara. But this is a limited view. Why should only one particular person among so many sentient beings be free from suffering? Wouldn't it be more worthwhile to think beyond ourselves and consider all the sentient beings who aspire to be happy just as we do?

We need to acknowledge our own wish to achieve happiness and avoid suffering, and realize that all sentient beings desire the same goals. We should be as concerned about others' well-being as we are about our own and endeavor to achieve our own enlightenment in order to free them from suffering and bring them happiness. The text admonishes us to consider our responsibility for bringing others to enlightenment by asking,

> Who is more shameless in this world,
> Than one who abandons to samsara's ocean of
> suffering

> All the mothers who have tenderly cared for him
>   since beginningless time
> And instead strives toward the peace of a solitary
>   nirvana?

In each of our lives since beginningless time, our mother carried us within her body for nine months. She took care of us when we were helpless babies; she gave us food, education, and protection. In return, we feel love and gratitude for her kindness.

Why not extend our respect and appreciation for our mother to everyone else? If we take a broader perspective, we can consider that, within the countless existences we have lived, every being has been our mother at one time or another. Don't they also deserve our kindness now? We can extend the same debt of gratitude that we owe our present mother to all sentient beings. By doing so, we naturally begin to develop a deep concern for the happiness of others, and this feeling makes sense to us.

We take the refuge vow not just for our own sake, but also for the sake of all sentient beings. This is bodhichitta, or the altruistic mind, which aims for the enlightenment of all sentient beings. This bodhichitta is so powerful and crucial to the path that the text says,

> For countless kalpas,
> Those with sublime intelligence and their heirs,
> Have investigated and seen with their mighty
>   wisdom
> That precious bodhichitta alone is of major benefit.

The supreme buddhas who have omniscient wisdom "and their heirs" are all the great male and female bodhisattvas who have followed in the Buddha's footsteps. They have realized that the sole reason for progressing on the path to enlightenment is the development of the altruistic attitude of bodhichitta. Strive to follow in their footsteps and develop the precious enlightened mind as they did.

There are two aspects to the actual training in bodhichitta: the relative and the absolute. Absolute bodhichitta is the realization of emptiness, which develops slowly in the course of time. Relative bodhichitta is an altruism rooted in loving-kindness and compassion. Relative bodhichitta manifests in attitude and in action. Cultivated in depth over a long period, the practice of relative bodhichitta will naturally transform your mind until absolute bodhichitta dawns.

RELATIVE BODHICHITTA

Relative bodhichitta is the aspiration to travel the path of enlightenment for the benefit of others. After generating this wish, you must train in it and put it into action, because

> If, among all the paths to the ultimate goal,
> You tread this one and open
> The treasury of the twofold aim,
> What other witness will you need?
>
> Following either of the two traditions,
> Generate bodhicitta as a vow and as an action;
> Learn its precepts, the detailed and the concise;
> The general and the specific,
> And put them earnestly into practice.

To "open the treasury of the twofold aim" means that by following this path, you will undoubtedly fulfill both your own aspirations and those of others. You can receive the transmission of the bodhisattva vow as a "witness" to your commitment. The two main traditions for this vow are the "vast" and the "profound." The Tradition of the Profound View came through the great

Nagarjuna, and the Tradition of Vast Activities was transmitted through Asanga. In both of these great lineages, the vow is to generate the thought of bodhichitta and put it into practice at all times. A sense of resolve must precede any endeavor so that you can commit yourself to accomplishing it. After taking the bodhisattva vow, you should begin by learning all the precepts and reaffirming your motivation, both general and specific. Then you start to apply your understanding earnestly in practice.

THE BENEFITS OF AWAKENING BODHICHITTA

> Consider the difference between the buddhas
> Who accomplish the benefit for others
> And we ordinary beings whose goal is our own
>   benefit.
> Even at the cost of your life, don't give up
>   bodhichitta.

Throughout our daily lives, we are preoccupied with our own self-centered motivations and what happens to us. Our main concern is securing our own welfare, usually at another's expense. We feel certain that we will find contentment by taking care of ourselves, but this is not the case. In fact, self-centeredness only increases our sufferings and creates an erratic pattern that causes us to swing between pleasure and suffering.

In contrast, the benefits of bodhichitta are clear. Those who became buddhas put others before themselves. Doing so is the secret to their success on the path to enlightenment. Their determination to be of benefit to others allows them to accomplish two goals: they help others, and at the same time, without trying, they achieve their own temporary and ultimate happiness.

The great deeds of the bodhisattvas might seem out of reach to you as a beginner. But by starting slowly, you will gradually be able to develop a capacity to manifest love and compassion.

Begin to develop a good heart by taking small steps. Try to be mindful so that even simple actions are not motivated by self-interest. By doing so, you will develop greater compassion.

> Since bodhichitta is the very root
> Of the oceanlike activity of the bodhisattvas,
> Know it to be the crux of all trainings,
> The root of the Mahayana path.

> If you have bodhichitta, you will go on the right
> path;
> All that you do, even neutral actions,
> Will turn into virtue,
> And you will never stray from the path of total
> liberation.

Bodhichitta should be at the root of all training and activities; this is the heart of the bodhisattva vow. Normally we do not associate neutral actions, such as washing clothes or climbing stairs, with any spiritual practice. But if your altruistic aim is to bring all sentient beings to enlightenment, bodhichitta will become second nature and permeate all of your thoughts and actions. It gives value to every aspect of life. With it, even the most insignificant, ordinary deed will bring you one step closer to achieving your goal, and you "will never stray from the path of total liberation."

> Without bodhichitta, whatever you do
> Will keep you on the lesser path;
> Even your virtuous deeds will perpetuate samsara,
> Not to speak of neutral and other deeds.
> Whatever you do, it will all be suffering.

Actions are neither intrinsically "good" nor "bad." Rather they become one or the other according to the motivation behind them. Constantly question whether your purpose for an act is unselfish or meant to cause further suffering. Do not simply look at the appearance of your actions and those of others, but consider the real reasons behind them. If you have bodhichitta, whatever you do will turn out positively. In contrast, if you do not have bodhichitta, you will remain "on the lesser path," and "even your virtuous deeds will perpetuate samsara." They might look good, but if they are not motivated by wanting to help others, they will not be beneficial to anyone.

> Therefore you must examine your mind again and
>   again
> With presence, awareness, and concern.
> Never think that it is a small offense
> To break the minor precepts.

Only by vigilantly questioning your motivation will you be able to determine whether it's self-centered or altruistic. The precepts require you to be selfless in all that you do. Do not think that minor transgressions don't matter, because they can result in even more destructive consequences. Be vigilant under all circumstances, even in the minutest aspects of life. This awareness is a key aspect for the development of bodhichitta. To give up the principle of altruistic mind is to lose the universal medicine that is essential to being "cured."

THE BODHISATTVA VOW

> Having asked the buddhas and bodhisattvas
> To give you their attention,
> You donned the armor of vowing to liberate
>   all beings,
> Thus gladdening gods and men.
> So if you deceive them now,
> What will become of all these sentient beings?

When taking the bodhisattva vow, you request the buddhas and bodhisattvas of the three times and ten directions to bear witness as you don the "armor" of courage and determination to liberate all beings. Nothing brings more joy to "gods and men" than when we dedicate ourselves to benefiting others. If you do not carry through with your promise, you will deceive and abandon not only yourself, but also the infinite number of sentient beings to whom you dedicated your efforts.

> It has been said that through perseverance
> Even bees and flies can achieve enlightenment.
> Why should you, a human being,
> Lack courage?

The immensity of this task (achieving enlightenment) might initially seem too daunting. You might feel discouraged and doubt your ability to fulfill your promise. But isn't becoming discouraged before you've even started just a form of laziness? The problem is not that the task is impossible, but your feeling that accomplishing the goal will require too much effort. In effect, you give up the race before even leaving the starting block.

We can counteract this inertia by remembering that we can accomplish anything with perseverance and determination. Innumerable beings have gradually progressed over many lifetimes from the state of animals to the human realm. Then after a long time as human beings, they persevered and achieved enlightenment. Even insects such as "bees and flies can achieve enlightenment." Why should we fall short now when we have all the necessary conditions for success that are inherent in a precious human life? As Shechen Gyaltsap says,

> With familiarity,
> Everything gets easier;
> Repeating your efforts over and over,
> You must train your mind.

The Tibetan word for meditation *(sgom pa)* means "familiarization." You can train your mind step by step and progress on the bodhisattva path. Time and effort are necessary before you can accomplish the most heroic deeds of the bodhisattva. So practice with perseverance and diligence. Make the vow and reflect on it during meditation, then try to put the aspiration into practice after meditation.

5

WORKING WITH AFFLICTIVE EMOTIONS

Among all the obscurations, the true root of samsara is our fixation on and attachment to the notion of self. As Chandrakirti said,

> First we cling to the notion of "I," then to the notion
>   of mine.
> I bow to the Great Compassionate One,
> Who has compassion for all those beings who
>   because of this clinging,
> Circle up and down in samsara as in a water mill.

Samsara begins when we delineate something as "the self" and grasp it as a truly existent entity. Obviously, positing an "I" brings about "the other," that which is not the "I." As a result, we begin differentiating between things—objects, possessions (that which is yours and mine), and so on—creating the duality of samsara and its subsequent suffering. A "Great Compassionate One," or someone who has achieved perfect understanding of the nondual nature of reality, cannot help but feel immense compassion for those who have fallen into this dualistic frame of mind.

> Although I have not done it the slightest harm,
> My enemy, ego-clinging,
> Has entrenched itself in my heart since
> beginningless time
> And confined me to the appalling prison of
> existence.

We consider an "enemy" to be someone who harms us, our belongings, or our loved ones. There are numerous ways to cope with or change our relationship with normal adversaries. We can retaliate and try to hurt them. We can try to win them over. We can make friends with them. We can try to resolve the situation through dialogue, by offering gifts, or by coming to a mutual compromise. Situations naturally change with time. Someone who was once our enemy can become our friend, and someone who has always been our friend can become our enemy.

But this is not the case with ego-clinging, which is a unique kind of enemy. Although we have done nothing to harm the ego, it has caused us continual harm since beginningless time. Ego-clinging is unrelenting. We cannot befriend it, nor can we seduce, bribe, convince, or establish fair terms with it. Unlike a normal enemy who needs to sleep, ego-clinging attacks twenty-four hours a day. It never gives us any respite. Whereas we can protect ourselves from a normal enemy and keep our distance, ego-clinging is at the very heart of our being, within our mind. Oddly enough, we have never turned away from it.

What can we do? First we must realize that grasping the ego has done us a great deal of harm. We must recognize the identity of the enemy and then vanquish it.

> It has inflicted hundreds of tortures upon me.
> Yet instead of resenting it,

> I have put my trust in it and fallen under its power.
> Is there any catastrophe, any delusion
> Worse than this?

The time is ripe to take action against ego-clinging. One way to free yourself from this enemy is to attack the notion of self and the afflicting mental states it engenders.

> Misplaced patience is contemptible.
> Taking the Three Jewels as my support,
> Mounting the horse of irrevocable renunciation,
> Donning the armor of the four boundless ones,
> And rallying the armies of the six paramitas,
> Today, with the sharp weapons of emptiness and
>   compassion,
> I shall slay my foe!

The metaphor of going to war when you can no longer tolerate an enemy describes the process of subduing the afflictive mental states by assailing them. To attack the enemy, we need allies. Of course, the strongest allies are the Three Jewels. If we trust the Buddha as our guide, the Dharma as the path, and the Sangha as our fellow warriors, we will become invincible.

To go into battle, we will need the strong "horse of irrevocable renunciation." Renunciation is the profound wish to escape from samsara forever. We will also need armor to protect us from weapons and shield us from negative emotions. Our finest armor is the practice of the four boundless meditations: (1) boundless loving-kindness, the wish that all sentient beings may have and know the causes of happiness; (2) boundless compassion, the wish that all sentient beings may be free of suffering and the causes of suffering; (3) boundless joy, the wish that any happiness sentient beings might already have will continually increase; and (4) boundless equanimity, the wish to apply the first three meditations equally and impartially to both friends and enemies.

Practicing these four boundless meditations attacks the enemies of jealousy, anger, pride, hatred, and attachment.

Our troops will be the six *paramitas* (transcendent perfections). Each of the paramitas is trained to defeat a particular enemy. Generosity vanquishes miserliness. Discipline conquers erratic conduct. Patience subdues anger. Diligence dispels laziness. Concentration overcomes distraction. Wisdom defeats ignorance and confusion. By defeating the enemy of ignorance, we will defeat all possible outer and inner enemies. These troops need weapons, the sharpest of which is emptiness imbued with compassion. Armed and confident, we will surely vanquish our foe.

> If I do not destroy ego-clinging,
> It will continue to generate the endless torments
> Of the hell Without Respite and others.
> What sane being would fail to take action?

Do not remain complacent in the face of this enemy who continues to cause you suffering. You must win the battle against the constant and repeated harm of ego-clinging. Failure to do so allows it to continue "to generate the never-ending torments" of samsara.

ABANDON NEGATIVE EMOTIONS BY INVESTIGATION

> Examine where the nature of the "self"
> Remains and goes to;
> You will discover that it does not possess the
>   slightest shred of existence.
> It is an enemy that, once subdued,
> Will never rise again.

For a long time we have believed in the existence of a solid, independent self. Now is the time to analyze this notion. We think of the self as a separate unit. In effect, we see it as the owner of our body and consciousness. We think "my name," "my body," "my mind" as if a separate, lasting self owned each. Let's examine that. Where is this self? Is it outside of us or associated with our body and mind? If it is in our body, in which part? We cannot find it.

When we investigate like this, we find that the self is just a concept. But where does this concept come from? Where does the self dwell if it is the consciousness that is present in our mind? Where does it go when it leaves? What happens to the self between past and future thoughts? Does the self dwell between two things that do not exist? How can the present thought of a self exist as something?

Consciousness is like a stream or river. We give a name to a river, as with the Ganges, because of its history and particular qualities. Yet this name is just a mental attribution for an ever-changing stream. We make a mistake when we think that the name implies some kind of permanent, fixed entity in the core of that dynamic stream. It's fine to label the river "Ganges." But nothing coming out of the river says, "I am the identity of the Ganges." It is the same for the self.

Once we realize that the self is a dynamic process and an attribution, we prevent ourselves from being fooled when strong mental factors associated with the notion of "I" arise. We slowly disentangle ourselves from confusion and dismount from the seesaw of hope and fear.

> In the past, the sublime, heroic bodhisattvas
> Achieved bliss by conquering this very enemy.
> Knowing the risks and benefits that are at stake,
> One who does not let this enemy escape
> Is the wisest of the wise,
> The bravest of the brave.
> Who can equal such a one?

Physical enemies can regroup after a defeat and attack again; not so with ego-clinging. This enemy will never arise again once you actually realize—not just intellectually—that it never truly existed in the first place. The great bodhisattvas of the past, who attained liberation by dissolving this grasping of the notion of self, provide the proof. Walk in their footsteps and accomplish this for yourself. By doing so, you will have won the ultimate battle against ignorance and suffering and accomplished the goal of the teachings.

THREE METHODS

> The wise Victorious Ones
> Expounded eighty-four thousand teachings
> To subdue ego-clinging,
> Tailored to the faculties of every being to be taught.

> All are for the single purpose of taming
> self-clinging.
> Depending on the level of one's intelligence,
> The obscuring emotions can be eradicated,
> transformed, or utilized.
> Yet in essence the root of all these
> Is the supreme training: bodhichitta.

All aspects of the Buddha's teachings target the eradication of clinging to the notion of self and reality. Ego-clinging assumes many forms as it pervades our mind and behavior. We need to employ various methods to attack it from different angles. Therefore the Buddha set forth eighty-four thousand teachings.

Basically, there are three ways to work with the afflictive emotions and their root, ego-clinging: you can discard, transform, or utilize them. Apply whichever method is most effective for your own nature and abilities. The safest method is to use direct antidotes to discard each afflictive emotion. This method works for everyone. Practitioners with some experience can use the second method to transform their emotions rather than counteract them with antidotes. Those with higher acumen and prowess can actually use the afflictive emotions as the path. In each case, the goal is always the same: to get rid of ego-clinging.

> How is one to practice?
> Not allowing free rein to ordinary thoughts
> That fabricate samsara,
> Master them with mindfulness.
> Recollect all your past anger
> And completely crush it with the army of the
>   antidotes:
> This is giving up the obscuring emotions.

Our thoughts and mental fabrications disturb us day and night. Like strong winds in a storm, they scatter our attention. Like thick clouds on a dark night, they obscure our true nature. They cannot bring us peace and only ensnare us further in suffering. We always give "free rein" to the various afflictive emotions such as desire, anger, hatred, pride, and jealousy. We permit them to invade our mind and proliferate. By doing so, we allow them to build into a strong force.

The first method Shechen Gyaltsap recommends for discarding these emotions is using an antidote to counteract them. A warrior prepares for battle by recalling all the harm that an enemy has caused. These thoughts provide the warrior with an incentive to vanquish his enemy.

You need to study your enemies. Use mindfulness to become aware of these negative thoughts as they arise. For example, when the first thought of anger arises, notice it and don't let it multiply. Instead, remember what happened in the past when you were overwhelmed by anger. Based on your direct experience, see the suffering and problems anger caused you and recognize its defects. You can crush anger using antidotes once you clearly see it as something destructive.

You can find a particular antidote to destroy each afflictive emotion. To conquer desire, you can meditate on the unappealing aspects of the object; for hatred, meditate on loving-kindness; for jealousy, joy; and so on. This is how you discard negative mental factors.

> Then to purify completely the entire field of your
> action,
> Like turning iron into gold,
> With relative bodhichitta, transform the three
> objects, the three poisons, and the three root
> merits.

The second method of handling negative emotions, appropriate for those of average ability, is to transform emotions as they arise. Once you are able to generate bodhichitta, the altruistic mind of enlightenment, you can apply it to all kinds of afflictive emotions. For example, use mindfulness to identify feelings of hatred when they arise, then think, "I am now experiencing animosity, which has caused me a lot of suffering in the past. May the animosity of all sentient beings be purified through my experience." Transform feelings of strong desire or anger as they arise by generating bodhichitta in exactly the same way.

Thoughts usually follow one another without pause. In the same way, we usually chase after our thoughts like a dog that fetches the same stick time after time. One thought gives birth to two, and two to three; soon they multiply and completely invade our mind. But unlike dogs, lions don't play fetch. Instead of watching the stick, a lion would turn back and look for the one who threw it. By following the lion's example, we can look for the source of our thoughts rather than following the thoughts themselves and see that they arise from the absolute nature of mind. With this process, thoughts naturally dissolve into that absolute nature and do not proliferate.

We can use relative bodhichitta to transform "the three objects, three poisons, and three root merits." The "three objects" are the concepts of a subject, the purpose of an action, and the action itself. The "three poisons" are hatred, desire, and mental confusion. The "three merits" are ordinary merits that are tainted with afflictive mental factors, ordinary merits that are free from such afflictions, and undetermined merits. These can be transformed into wisdom by applying bodhichitta.

> Finally, practicing absolute bodhichitta,
> Realize that whatever arises is the display of
> dharmakaya,
> The primordial nature, unbroken simplicity.
> Without clinging, whatever arises is naturally freed.
> In the great equal taste without rejecting or
> accepting,
> Continue on.

> The meaning, the primordial indivisibility of
> wisdom and skillful means,
> Emptiness with compassion as its very essence,
> Must be carried onto the path.

In the third method, practitioners of the highest capacity use their afflictive emotions as part of the path to enhance the realization of emptiness. Look at the actual nature of those afflictions. All thoughts and emotions are the play of the primordial nature, or the *dharmakaya*. They arise within it and dissolve back into it. When we recognize this, no matter what mental event arises, we see it as arising from the dharmakaya and dissolving back into it. We also recognize that thoughts never have come into existence, remain, or cease. They will no longer trouble us. Whatever arises will naturally be freed because we see its primordial nature.

The ability to recognize emptiness as the true nature of thoughts—and consequently liberate them as they arise—eliminates the need to reject each thought with a specific antidote. This is the meaning of the "great equal taste."

Our aim should be to reach a level of realization that unites the wisdom of emptiness with the spontaneously present skillful means of compassion. That's why the text says, "emptiness with compassion as its very essence." We must carry this on the path and apply it in every stage of practice for the duration of our lives. Recognizing the emptiness of thoughts instead of solidifying them allows the arising and subsiding of each thought to clarify and strengthen the realization of emptiness.

6

THE SUBLIME EXCHANGE OF HAPPINESS AND SUFFERING

However, to gradually gain steadiness of mind,
Beginners must first practice relative bodhichitta.

To gain a steady and stable mind, first practice relative bodhichitta. Begin by considering others as equal to you and then put yourself in their place and vice versa. After you develop sufficient strength and courage, continue to train by putting the happiness of others above your own.

To do this, know that all sentient beings have been
   your mother,
Ponder their kindness and think of a way to repay it.

Throughout countless existences, we have all been related to each other in a multitude of ways. At one time or another, every single being has been your mother. An acute awareness of personal connection to all other beings throughout many lifetimes promotes a vast sense of interdependence that will make your loving-kindness practice universal and unlimited.

Regardless of how you may feel about your present mother, try to acknowledge her generosity. I have heard some people say that they cannot feel a debt of gratitude to their mother because of past grievances. They say they would rather meditate on their dog or cat! But our pets do not bring us into this world; our mothers do. Loving your pets is wonderful, but that is another issue.

Your mother invested a great deal of kindness and patience when she carried you, a tiny stranger, in her womb for nine months. After you were born, you still needed her to survive. You were like an Unidentified Crying Object whom she fed and clothed. She gave you life and nurtured you out of kindness. At the most basic level, you simply would not be alive without your mother. As you grew, she may have done much more to care for you and teach you how to survive in the world.

No matter what later happened in life, try to experience gratitude for her initial kindness so that you will naturally want to repay her by bringing her happiness. Practice extending that same gratitude and respect to all sentient beings, no matter what your current relationship with them is. Concern for the happiness of others can begin to arise naturally when you consider them with the same affection and gratitude that you have for the person who gave you this present life.

> Develop gentle love and the rest of the four
> boundless qualities,
> Especially the miraculous great compassion.

> Meditating stage by stage upon the objects
> Toward which these four arise very easily,
> Relatively easily, and with difficulty,
> Train yourself in these four immeasurables through
> various methods.

> Since one cannot make absolute judgments,
> You and all beings are equal in wanting happiness;
> You and all beings are equal in wanting to avoid
>   suffering.

Since generating love and compassion for people you do not know or like is difficult, at first you need to develop these feelings slowly, step-by-step. Begin by arousing feelings of tenderness and loving-kindness for those close to you. Then let those feelings become more vivid and present in your mind. Over time they will grow until they overflow to complete strangers, and then to people for whom you feel animosity. Why exclude anyone?

Someone who was once a friend can become an enemy and someone who was once an enemy can become a friend. In fact, someone you have thought of as an enemy throughout this lifetime may have been your best friend or favorite relative in a past life. How can you ascribe such notions as "enemy" or "friend" to anyone when the situation is constantly changing? The aim of loving-kindness is that all beings find happiness; no one is excluded. Try to wish that everyone achieves well-being and happiness.

Persevere in this practice, repeating it again and again, step-by-step, for each of "the four boundless qualities": loving-kindness, compassion, sympathetic joy, and equanimity. Begin with whichever quality arises most naturally in your mind, and start with those people you care most about. Then extend it to those you think of as being more difficult, to strangers or even adversaries. Feeling love and compassion for people you do not like is difficult, but there are many strategies that can help change that attitude. First remember that everyone—friend and enemy alike—strives for happiness and wants to avoid suffering. When you see people busy with their daily affairs, recognize that their activities stem from a wish to find fulfillment. No one goes to all that trouble just to suffer! Understand that your enemy wants happiness just as you do.

Wish others happiness even if they have a negative attitude toward you or wrongly harm you out of ignorance. The understanding that all beings have exactly the same rights to happiness will allow you to approach others with a sense of impartiality. You will realize that there is no reason why your happiness should come before theirs. If you continue to practice with this in mind, you will reach the next step—putting yourself in another's place. It is simply a matter of time.

The idea of sacrificing someone else's happiness for your own becomes out of the question once you open your eyes to the equality of all sentient beings and erase the line dividing them from you. For example, imagine that one of your fingers became infected and needed to be amputated. Would it make sense to cling to that one finger at the risk of losing your whole hand? Of course not. Then why are people so doubtful when it comes to themselves and others? In the case of your hand, you distinctly feel a sense of interdependence and unity. It's easy to understand that the whole hand is more important than a part. Having a sense of genuine equality with others will help you to put their needs ahead of your own, thereby breaking the barrier of self-centeredness.

Skillful training in the development of all four boundless attitudes develops this sense of equality. Be careful not to get stuck in only one of them. For example, when you focus on loving-kindness, you might drift toward grasping and attachment. If this happens, shift to compassion and focus on the intense suffering of all sentient beings. But all this suffering might overwhelm you by creating a sense of powerlessness and depression. If that happens, look at others' happiness or good qualities and rejoice in them. Wish that their happiness will increase even more and that all unhappiness and despair will be dispelled. If you then get carried away by rejoicing and happiness and develop an unrealistic assessment of the true condition of beings, switch to equanimity or impartiality by developing a feeling of love and compassion for all. The process of alternating from one quality to another enables you to progress without getting trapped in any deviations.

THE PRACTICE OF EXCHANGING

> In order to become used to caring for others more
>   than yourself,
> You should bring to mind the essential points and
>   integrate in your being
> The visualizations for exchanging self and others,
> While riding the horse of the breath.

There is a wondrous method of exchanging yourself for others that uses a breathing technique. It can help to instill the four boundless qualities in your true nature. Nothing is more natural than breathing. As long as we are alive, we breathe.

In this practice, breathe out while thinking, "May all my good qualities, happiness, merit, and realization go out with my breath and benefit all beings." Think that all beings receive these benefits. Then breathe in while imagining that you inhale all of their suffering and its causes, their negative thoughts, and so on. Imagine that you attract these afflictions and negativities like a magnet, and by dissolving all that you inhale into your heart, others are freed. Then while briefly holding your breath, transform all the suffering and negativity that you inhaled into joy and happiness.

By repeating this again and again, it will become natural to wish others happiness and to take their suffering upon yourself. Maintaining this practice in all circumstances is a powerful means for developing the four boundless qualities.

Some people might think that they cannot do this practice

because they already suffer too much. If you feel like this, use another visualization. Imagine a sphere of brilliant light in the center of your heart. The light is the bodhichitta, the courage of compassion. Gather the sufferings and mental poisons of all sentient beings into the form of a gray mass or cloud that disappears into this brilliant sphere of light and is totally purified. This will transform both your own sufferings and that of others without giving you a sense of being burdened by their suffering.

You can vary this by visualizing your body as a sapphire, a wish-fulfilling jewel that radiates light to all sentient beings and gives them everything they wish for or need while freeing them from suffering. Or you can imagine that your body can multiply and change into hundreds of forms. Each form goes to all sentient beings and transforms into whatever they need. For those in need of food, it becomes food. For those who need clothing, it becomes clothing. Through these limitless forms, you are able to fulfill the infinite needs of beings.

> Do not count this practice,
> Nor measure it in terms of days, months, or years.
> Ask whether true experience has been born within
>   or not
> And be sincere in making bodhichitta an
>   all-embracing,
> Profound, integral part of yourself.

You should not measure this practice by keeping count of how many times you do it as if you were manufacturing something in a factory. Nor should you practice for only a few months and then forget it and move on to something else. Do not approach it as if you were studying to qualify for a certificate. Instead, you need to understand that repetition, familiarization, cultivation, and meditation are the path to achieving a true experience of bodhichitta.

True experience is not limited to formal meditation sessions.

You still have work to do if, after meditating, you feel just as angry and impatient as you did before the session. You need to get to a point where compassion and bodhichitta are second nature and there is no difference between meditation and daily life. Strive to be like an accomplished equestrian who maintains balance without thinking even when the horse is galloping at full speed and leaping over obstacles.

Dilgo Khyentse Rinpoche always used to emphasize the importance of unifying the practice and your life. He said, "It is not when things go well that you can judge a true practitioner. But when adverse circumstances arise, then you can clearly see the shortcomings of the practice." Mind training should become an integral part of your ongoing experience, a practice that you can apply whatever the conditions. When this happens, difficult circumstances will not dishearten you nor will favorable ones elevate you. Check repeatedly to see whether your way of being and the teachings have become one and whether you can apply them in any situation.

Enhancement of the Practice: Accumulation of Merit, Dedication, and Rejoicing

> In order to weaken whatever contradicts this
> practice
> And to strengthen whatever assists it,
> You should, to the utmost of your ability,
> Purify your obscurations, perfect the accumulations,
> And pray repeatedly to the guru and the Three
> Jewels,
> Putting all your hopes in them.

You need to overcome the attitudes and habits that so often contradict your practice. Using skillful means to transform ordinary activities into opportunities for developing bodhichitta strengthens the practice and quickens the journey. For example, apply the benefits of positive practices such as making offerings, performing prostrations and circumambulations, and reciting mantras to a larger goal than your own limited, selfish purposes. Always dedicate the merit with thoughts such as, "May I dedicate this practice for the benefit of others. May all beings develop bodhichitta, the vast enlightened mind." Doing so will broaden the scope of your actions.

To progress you need to have confidence in those who have already developed the qualities you are seeking and who are, therefore, worthy of that confidence. Do not place your trust in ordinary, confused people. This is why we take refuge in the Buddha, Dharma, and Sangha. The Buddha symbolizes enlightenment; the Dharma, his teachings; and the Sangha, the community of all who follow in his footsteps. In addition, perceiving your own guru as a Buddha is of the utmost importance.

> When your own happiness increases
> Or when you simply have desire for it,
> You must understand that virtuous deeds lead to
>   happiness.

> Therefore at all times gather your energy
> And generously dedicate it to all sentient beings,
> Praying that your happiness and virtuous deeds
> May nurture all beings.

Happiness and suffering are manifestations of the law of cause and effect. They are not gifts or curses that arbitrarily happen to fall upon us. Virtue and nonvirtue are the causes of happiness and suffering. Virtuous actions bring about happiness, and nonvirtuous ones create suffering. When an experience of happiness arises, rejoice in it as the accumulation of virtuous deeds. When you experience suffering, realize that it is purely a result of your own actions.

Dedicate whatever happiness you enjoy to all sentient beings, wishing that whatever you have gained from your own virtuous actions will help nurture and serve everyone. All that you do and experience, all your happiness and suffering, should lead to the development of bodhichitta. Your confidence should become so firm that you are able to accept both life and death with equanimity.

> When you see others acting virtuously,
> Rejoice from your heart,
> Without animosity or jealousy,
> And pray that everyone may act likewise.

Appreciating the happiness and virtue of others is an essential part of bodhichitta. When we see others enjoying happiness, engaging in spiritual practice, or performing acts of generosity or other virtuous deeds, we can react in one of two ways. We can either rejoice or feel disturbed. Fully rejoicing in other people's virtues allow us to share in their merit immediately and with very little effort. On the other hand, feeling jealous or upset by another's happiness merely creates negative feelings and plants the seeds for further suffering. Therefore it is very important to appreciate the happiness and virtue of others.

7

THE ROOT OF SUFFERING

The next section of the text concerns the need to identify the cause of suffering as our strong grasping of the notion of a self. To dissolve or get rid of that grasping, we must understand that

> When undesirable things come to pass
> Or when you simply wish to be rid of sufferings,
> You must understand that these are proof
> That their cause, nonvirtue, must be eliminated.
> Mustering the four powers,
> Attack the one responsible: ego-clinging.

As explained in the last chapter, suffering does not randomly appear nor is it imposed on us by external gods or demons. Suffering is simply a result of our past actions. Therefore, to alleviate suffering and prevent it from arising again, we must look at its root causes: nonvirtuous thoughts and actions.

We must identify suffering and sever its root. What are the "four powers" that can transform nonvirtuous actions? The first is the power of regret, or the awareness that it would be much wiser not to indulge in thoughts, words, and actions that cause suffering. Regret teaches us something; it is not like guilt, which leaves us powerless. With regret, we understand how we have caused suffering to others and ourselves through mental afflictions based on ego-clinging. This type of regret analyzes the causes of suffering and acts as a remedy to ignorance, the root of ego-clinging.

The second power is the power of a support that will help us mend our mistaken ways. The Buddha or a spiritual teacher is an excellent support for this transformation. The third power is the power of the antidote. In this case, the antidote is a method of purification, such as the practice of Vajrasattva. Antidotes also include performing positive actions and confession. The fourth power is the firm determination to refrain from further nonvirtuous actions and thoughts.

> Pray that all the degeneration and faults,
> Which are the causes, conditions, and results
> Of the suffering of an infinite number of beings,
> May ripen upon you,
> And that all beings may become free of their
> sufferings,
> Which are but the result of their own negative
> actions.

There is a positive aspect to suffering; it acts as a reminder of the law of cause and effect. It is also a catalyst that increases our compassion. It provides an occasion for us to exchange our own happiness for the suffering of others. We can make this wish: "Let me make use of this suffering. Through my suffering, may the sufferings of others be alleviated. May all beings be free of suffering and enjoy happiness."

> Especially whenever any of the five poisonous
> emotions,

Or any of the eight worldly concerns arise,
Seize hold of them with fresh presence of mind.

Afflictive mental states, such as desire, hatred, and pride, poison our mind and destroy any happiness we may experience. They are the cause of our preoccupation with the eight worldly concerns—pain and pleasure, gain and loss, fame and anonymity, and praise and blame—that keep us torn between hope and fear, doubt and hesitation. These eight worldly concerns and the afflictive emotions have ruled our thoughts for a long time, but now is the moment to find a "fresh presence of mind."

First, we must recognize these mental states. A thief in your home who escapes notice can continue to steal your belongings. You make it more difficult for the thief to steal from you again as soon as you become aware of his presence. Likewise, applying mindfulness and vigilance to recognize destructive mental factors or emotions enables you to catch them as they arise. By catching them early, you have a better chance of not getting carried away by them.

"Seize hold of the emotions with mindfulness," Dilgo Khyentse Rinpoche used to say, "Hold the spear of mindfulness at the door of the citadel of the mind and proclaim, 'If you, the enemy of obscuring emotions intensify your presence, I will intensify my vigilance. Only when you disappear, will I relax my own vigilance.'"

As a mental exercise to vanquish ego-clinging,
Recollect all the times you have been wronged.
First think of all the obscuring emotions
And the notion that beings and phenomena truly
    exist,
Which create obstacles to the higher aspirations
Of all beings in general and of Dharma practitioners
    in particular,

> And the difficulties and adversities arising from
>   these.
>
> Then gather all of them with your inhalation,
> Dissolve it into your own ego-clinging,
> And destroy the curse itself.
> Gather into one essential point
> A fierce determination to eliminate ego-clinging
> Together with its antidote
> And the meditation practice that averts it.

The source of the five obscuring emotions, the eight worldly concerns, and all the afflictive mental factors is ego-clinging. The purpose of all Dharma practice is to destroy the curse of grasping to an ego.

Once you clearly identify the root of the problem, you should make a fierce resolution to eradicate it immediately. Perhaps you think that bringing everything back to ego-clinging is oversimplifying the matter. But simple though it seems, ego-clinging or self-importance *is* the source of all our problems. This is the essential point of all aspects of the practice.

There is a specific practice that can be done to help overpower the feeling of self-importance. First, inhale all the obstacles, difficulties, and adversities with your breath. Let them hit your feeling of self-importance like cannonballs until it crumbles like dust. Then enjoy the freedom and lightness of being liberated from the prison of ego-clinging.

> This is what propels the practice.
> Though seemingly insignificant, it is the very crux
> And brings the greatest progress on the path.
> That is the relative mind training.

You will make great progress on the path if you focus on dissolving your clinging to the notion of self. This is what the essence of training in relative bodhichitta, or "relative mind training," is all about.

Develop a genuine sense of compassion and loving-kindness so that boundless love will rule your heart. This feeling should not be fleeting and superficial, but something that motivates all your actions. Have the courage to vow to dedicate all your efforts to attain enlightenment in order to free countless beings from suffering.

In *The Way of the Bodhisattva,* Shantideva writes,

> Since it is said,
> "There is immeasurable virtue
> In wanting to cure even the mildest headache of a
>   single being.
> What about wanting to dispel
> All of the sufferings of all sentient beings?" [9]

8

STAGES OF TRAINING IN THE ULTIMATE AWAKENED MIND

Absolute bodhichitta is the subject of the second main section of the teachings. The two aspects of bodhichitta—the relative and the absolute—are fundamentally not distinct entities, but two aspects of understanding and realization that reinforce each other, like the two wings of a bird work together to make flight possible.

All sentient beings want to be free from suffering and achieve happiness. However, they are confused about how to accomplish these aims. Ironically, their actions often contradict their desire, continually perpetuating suffering and destroying any chance for happiness. A natural, profound compassion arises in us once we realize this human condition.

Yet simply having this feeling of compassion is not enough. We actually need to *do* something to benefit others. The supreme way to be of benefit is to dispel the cause of suffering—ignorance. To do this, we must progress toward enlightenment, and for that, we need to develop a profound understanding of the absolute truth.

ABSOLUTE BODHICHITTA

> Once you grow familiar with this,
> Develop absolute bodhichitta.

Three kinds of knowledge eventually help us to understand the absolute truth: the knowledge of hearing or studying; the knowledge that is born from deeply contemplating what has been heard or studied; and the knowledge gained from meditating or becoming familiar through experience with what was heard and reflected upon. By progressing through these three types of knowledge, we gain insight through direct experience into the absolute aspect of the awakened mind. We become more familiar with the nature of the inner phenomena of mind and the outer phenomena of appearances.

Ignorance is the root of our strong tendency to perceive things as pleasant, unpleasant, or neutral. Our judgments of beauty or ugliness lead us to attribute those characteristics directly to an outer object. We begin to discriminate by accepting what we like and rejecting what we dislike.

> All discernible appearances, both outer and inner
>   phenomena,
> Are like dreams and illusions—
> In the past they did not exist,
> In the end they will not exist,
> And in between they appear through a chain of
>   interdependent factors.

Dreams of drowning or being consumed by flames can be very vivid and frightening. While we are in the midst of the experience we have no way of knowing that our dreams are not real. Only when we wake up do we realize that it was nothing more than a manifestation of our own mind. The way we normally perceive phenomena as pleasant or unpleasant is similar to dreaming.

Appearances, like dreams, are devoid of any intrinsic existence. They come from nothing and leave nothing behind, no matter how long they last. How can they appear if they are devoid of intrinsic existence? In fact, they can manifest in an infinite number of ways, such as a rainbow that appears only through the temporary combination of many factors. These factors can come together precisely because they do not exist autonomously and are not endowed with a permanent reality. No phenomenon exists alone, and none has a solid existence.

Appearances become more transparent and less solid as we familiarize ourselves with seeing phenomena as dreams and illusions.

> Although they appear,
> From the very beginning phenomena are empty of
>   true existence;
> Intrinsically, they are without essence,
> Nor do they remain.
> The expression is the kayas and wisdoms,
> Yet the absolute nature never changes:
> As it was, so it shall be.

The phenomenal world is just like a dream. Phenomena appear solid, but they do not exist in the same way as they appear. There is no solid reality behind them; from the very beginning, they are empty of intrinsic existence. There is nothing but a dynamic stream of ever-changing, interdependent relationships.

There are two ways to view phenomena. The first is with "impure" vision. This is the deluded way of perceiving everything as solid and attributing essential qualities to it. The second is to recognize the unchanging, empty nature of all phenomena.

Phenomena are an expression of the kayas and wisdoms.

The *kayas* are the different dimensions of buddhahood—manifested, subtle, and absolute. Wisdom is the natural mode of the mind when it is not deluded. Whether or not phenomena appear, the absolute nature does not change. The absolute nature is not the absence of phenomena, but their very nature.

> Not knowing this, childish sentient beings
> Treat phenomena as if they were solid and real.
> Thus begins a chain of attractions and aversions
> And the great sufferings of this existence—
> a nonexistent masquerade!

If we recognize the unchanging, absolute nature of phenomena, we also recognize their intangibility. Things appear yet are empty; they are empty yet appear. Emptiness is not the absence of phenomena, and phenomena are not the absence of emptiness. Rather, there is a union of appearance and emptiness. Having just a glimmer of understanding that things are not as they appear is a big step toward seeing the true nature of things.

We are like naïve children who are easily fooled by appearances until we gain this understanding. In our confusion, we treat the phenomenal world as solid and real. We do not see that it is merely an expression of wisdom and the display of emptiness. We reify phenomena and set in motion an unending succession of attractions and aversions that lead to craving and desire. This one mistake—solidifying phenomena—gives rise to the endless cycle of samsara, which is why all the suffering of existence is just a "nonexistent masquerade."

> The powerful roots are ignorance
> And assuming that beings and phenomena truly
> exist,
> When these become habitual,
> Conditioned existence arises.

Our ignorant habit of misconstruing the phenomenal world as solid leads to grasping at reality, which is the root of samsara. The more we grasp, the more solid phenomena seem. This long-standing habit is difficult to change. Our grasping is like an old piece of parchment paper that has been rolled up for years. When we try to lay it flat, it immediately rolls up again. Over time, the parchment can eventually be flattened. Likewise, we need time to disentangle ourselves from grasping reality. We need to reflect and investigate the nature of self and phenomena again and again so we can gradually come to this understanding.

> Following the scriptures and the guru's pith
>   instructions,
> Fortunate beings who aspire to freedom
> Must first acquaint themselves
> With the nonexistence of beings and phenomena.

To dispel our ordinary delusions, we should follow the authentic scriptures, heed a qualified teacher's oral instructions, and try to put them both into practice. Combining these two aspects is important. The scriptures are authentic reasoning and cognition based on the profound understanding of the Buddha and his followers. The profound pith instructions of the guru are based on experience. The guru can help us have a direct experience of what the teachings are actually describing.

IDENTIFYING THE OBJECT OF CLINGING

> Clinging to the notion that a self actually exists
> Is taking the thought of "I" to be an actual entity
> And results from a mistaken apprehension
> Of the perishable five aggregates.

The "I" is a transitory collection of the five aggregates, which constitute our psychophysical system. We mistakenly take the gathering of mind and body—the skandhas of form, feeling, perception, mental formation, and consciousness—to be the self. The aggregates are, in essence, multiple and ephemeral. Yet we create the idea of a self that is whole and perpetual. Ego-clinging is the concept of a distinct "I" that we superimpose on these aggregates.

> If one examines properly
> The collection of these five aggregates—
> Which are multiple and impermanent,
> Like lightning, a waterfall, or a butter lamp—
> One sees, as when mistaking a rope for a snake,
> That the self is nothing but a misperception:
> It is nonexistent, devoid of intrinsic reality.

We need to deconstruct our notion of self. When we say "I" or the self, we think of a lasting and united entity. But in fact, that "I" is only a collection of aggregates, and these aggregates are ephemeral and change every instant like a waterfall or the flame of a butter lamp. A waterfall appears to be continuous, but it is actually composed of an ever-changing flow of drops of water. Likewise, the flame of a butter lamp is just a continuous series of flickers of light rather than a permanent flame.

Examining and analyzing our perceptions is essential. In the dark, we can easily mistake a coil of rope for a snake and become frightened. But upon investigation, we discover that there never was a snake. All the fear and dread we felt came from our misperception of the rope as a snake. The fear disappears as soon as we recognize our mistake. We were frightened, but experiencing that fear did not turn the rope into a snake. Likewise, if we properly examine the self, we discover that it does not truly exist. We are not getting rid of anything; the self simply did not exist in the first place. It is nothing but a misperception.

When we say, "Someone pushed me," it indicates that we associate ourselves with the body. When we say, "I'm sad," we are associating the "I" with the mind. This places the self in two different locations. So where is the "I"? Is there a specific "I" in the body? Since we are unable to find it, we generally associate the "I" with a kind of mental or physical experience.

What is that experience? Past thoughts are gone; future ones have not yet arisen. The stream of consciousness is just a succession of present moments. So how can anything be permanent or exist separately when these moments disappear?

The feeling of "I" is natural as long as we do not believe it denotes a permanent entity. It is legitimate to give the label "I" to a continuous stream of consciousness that is a constantly changing dynamic process. That process has characteristics and its own history. We can call it "I" if we know that is merely a name, just as we call a river by a name according to its characteristics. But as we mentioned in chapter 5, the river is understood to be a changing phenomenon. No one thinks that if we call "Ganges," a small head will come out of the river saying, "That's me. I am the Ganges." Likewise, there is no "I" swimming in the stream of consciousness.

In the same way, the idea of "mine" is just a label. Let's examine how labeling phenomena as "mine" transforms the way we perceive things. Imagine that you are looking in a shop window at a beautiful and expensive vase. Then a cat knocks the vase over, and it breaks. You think, "What a pity. It was such a nice vase," and you go on walking. Now imagine that a friend has given you an expensive vase. It is on your mantel, and your cat knocks it down. You say, "*My* vase is broken! Oh, no!" and that is a catastrophe, simply because of the label "mine" that you put on the vase. The label made a big difference.

ESTABLISHING THE EMPTINESS OF INNER AND OUTER PHENOMENA

> Clinging to the notion that phenomena truly exist
> Is clinging to the notion of subject and object.

All the objects one apprehends, outer and inner
  phenomena,
Are illusory appearances resulting from habitual
  tendencies.

Like visual aberrations,
Like reflections of the moon on water, and like
  mistaken perceptions,
When unexamined they are taken for granted;
When examined they are seen to be nothing at all.

Just as we found that our personal identity has no true existence, we also need to examine the nature of outer phenomena to determine whether they are also empty. We habitually accept phenomena as they appear. The world seems solid because we do not analyze what we see. By carefully examining external phenomena, such as houses, we discover that they too have no inherent existence. A house is a composite of parts made up of atoms. But a proper analysis of atoms reveals that, no matter how small they are, no indivisible particles of matter truly exist. By probing like this, we find that there is an absence of identity in everything.

The appearance of phenomena is inseparable from emptiness. The interplay of emptiness and appearance is like the example of the reflection of the moon on water. To think that the moon is actually in the water is a mistaken perception. The reflection can be seen, but it is empty of a solid moon.

The main point of the union of appearance and emptiness is that emptiness is not the absence of phenomena, but the absence of its nature. That is why things can appear in so many different ways even though they are devoid of intrinsic reality. The inseparability of appearance and emptiness is the most essential and direct way of describing reality.

Phenomena are not definable entities
As atoms and seconds would be.

> Therefore you must conclude that subject and object
> Cannot in any way be said to exist.

All phenomena are constantly changing. They never remain the same for even an instant. However, in our distorted perception, we do not notice the constant occurrence of minute transformations. We must therefore conclude that both external objects and the grasping mind that perceives them have no fixed inherent existence.

> By continuously turning the wheel of investigation,
> You will gain confidence
> In the nonexistence of both beings and phenomena
> And a time will come when you achieve certainty
> That the two truths,
> The illusory arising of interdependent events
> And the emptiness that is devoid of all assumptions,
> Are not contradictory but, in essence, one.

Analyze the personal self as well as phenomena until you are certain of their inherently empty nature. When you have truly taken this to heart, you will fully understand that the two truths are essentially one. They are not two separate things like the horns of a bull. Absolute truth is the ultimate nature of all phenomena, and relative truth is how all phenomena appear. The ordinary, deluded mind perceives a difference between the way things seem and their true nature. But at the end of your journey, you will directly perceive the ultimate nature of phenomena in which all disparity between appearance and reality vanishes.

It is said by the Kadampa masters that "even if you do not have a complete understanding of emptiness, if just a genuine doubt regarding the solidity of phenomena arises in your mind, this thought has the power to turn the delusion of samsara into dust."

When I was in Los Angeles, I visited a film studio and saw the sets. Everything—the houses, the streets, and so on—looked so real from the front. But when I walked around to the back of the buildings, I saw that nothing was there. They were empty. I visited a hospital set and saw doctors and nurses walking around as if it were a real hospital. I was wearing my monks' robes, and an actor came up to me and said, "Are you real?" Now when I watch movies, I keep remembering that there is nothing behind the facades, and I don't get so emotionally involved.

> When all preconceptions that assert separation
> Between manifestation and emptiness collapse,
> Investigation comes to an end.
> Then what is the use of conceptual reasoning?

The certainty that both beings and phenomena lack an inherent self, which we gain through investigation, will allow us to realize that phenomena appear through interdependent origination. Like a dream or mirage, they appear as the results of complex relationships between countless causes and conditions, none of which truly exist.

We will stop clinging to notions of subject and object once we understand the nonduality of appearance and emptiness. At that point, we will no longer need to analyze these concepts.

A MISTAKEN VIEW OF EMPTINESS

> Emptiness is the antidote to all views,
> But if one clings to the concept of emptiness,
> Like a purgative turned into poison,
> It becomes ineffective.

Clinging to the concept of emptiness can be quite dangerous. For instance, imagine that you are sick and there is only one remedy for your illness. If you do not follow the prescription properly, the illness will get worse and you will have spoiled your only chance for a cure. Emptiness is the best cure for your mistaken clinging to the reality of phenomena. But if you cling to the concept of emptiness, it will cease to be the remedy and provide no benefit, and you will lose the opportunity to be cured.

> Like two sticks that when rubbed together
> Are consumed in the fire of their own making,
> The antidote itself must disappear of its own accord.

Once you have started a fire by rubbing two sticks together, there is no further use for the sticks. Use emptiness to subdue your clinging, and then simply rest in the true nature of emptiness. In this way, you will encounter the absolute nature that has been present from the very beginning, free of object and reference point.

9

THE GREAT PERFECTION

Relax in the continuum of primordial simplicity,
Which is the absolute nature that remains since the
  beginning,
The natural state, the expanse endowed with the
  three doors of liberation:
Emptiness, absence of characteristics, and absence of
  intent.

The natural state of emptiness is endowed with "three doors of liberation": (1) its essence or nature is empty; (2) its cause is free from mental elaborations or conventional characteristics; (3) and the fruit is not "something" to be obtained, but rather a state of wisdom to be actualized. We should rest, uncontrived and relaxed, within that state.

Then you will see the radiant buddha-nature,
In which all fabrications and workings of mind
Are at peace in the absolute expanse.

When the meaning of emptiness is perfectly realized, the

entity called mind—together with all its mental events and elaborations—will naturally be pacified. The cessation of all conceptual thought is the dharmakaya. Ignorance, its delusions, and the resulting mental constructions all must cease in order to stabilize this wisdom that is beyond concepts. When these fabrications vanish in the absolute expanse, the fundamental nature of the mind is realized.

UNITING APPEARANCES AND EMPTINESS

> Empty by nature, it is free from eternalism;
> Cognizant in its expression, it is free from nihilism.
> Although one thus considers two aspects,
> It is the basic nature in which
> All notions of dualistic perception are freed in their
> own space:
> Inconceivable, ineffable, apprehended by wisdom
> alone,

The buddha-nature is void in character and luminous in expression. It is a state of realization, not an entity endowed with intrinsic reality. It is free from the concepts of existing and not existing. It is not an eternal being. By recognizing this, we will not fall into the mistaken view of externalism.

"Empty by nature" does not mean that it is nothingness or a complete void. It is "cognizant in its expression" because it manifests as boundless enlightened qualities. By realizing this cognizant, luminous aspect, we counteract the danger of falling into the extreme view of nihilism.

The empty and cognizant natures of buddhahood are one. Emptiness and appearance occur together without contradiction. This great equality in which there are no dividing concepts is indescribable. It cannot be experienced with the ordinary intellect, but only by the wisdom of self-existing awareness.

> Uncompounded by nature,
> Seen without seeing,
> As when gazing into vajra space,
> It is called "seeing the sky of the absolute."

When we look at the sky, we say that we see space, but actually there is nothing to see. Seeing the absolute nature is a way of seeing without the split between that which is seen, the one who sees, and the act of seeing. This inconceivable wisdom is uncompounded. It is like "vajra space"—the expanse of pure awareness that is free of something to be seen and something that sees. "Seen without seeing" indicates that we have recognized the ultimate nature.

> There is nothing to dispel
> Nor the slightest thing to add.
> Looking perfectly at perfection itself,
> Seeing perfection, one is perfectly liberated.

Nothing needs to be eliminated from or added to the tathagatagarbha. Nothing can spoil it, just as clouds cannot change the actual light of the sun. Emotional obscurations are just extraneous veils that never penetrate or spoil the primordially perfect and unchanging buddha-nature. It simply rests naturally as it is. When we look without dualistic clinging ("perfectly") at the buddha-nature ("perfection itself"), we will be "liberated."

> When tangible things and intangible things
> Cease to remain present in the mind,
> In the absence of other alternatives,
> Naked of all concepts, this is complete peace.

Once we can perceive in actuality that neither substantial nor insubstantial things truly exist, we will be free of any reference points and grasping reality. Our mind will not be torn apart by dualistic perceptions and will be perfectly peaceful.

> Unaware of this vital point,
> To painfully nail down your mind
> With mental fabrications is not calm-abiding;
> To construct intellectual boundaries is not insight.

This verse is a quote from the ninth chapter of the *Way of the Bodhisattva*. The practice of *shamatha* ("calm-abiding") meditation is directed at making the mind stable and clear. Our present mind is like a pot of boiling water—agitated, bubbling, and swirling around. In order to catch a glimpse of the real nature of the mind, it is often necessary to begin by calming unruly thoughts and making the mind more serene.

To see the bottom of a lake, we need to stop stirring up the mud below. We also need to let the mud of wild and discursive thoughts settle down. When this happens, the mind will naturally become transparent. We will then be able to see far into the mind's depths and perceive its true nature.

Being guided toward the inconceivable nature through calm-abiding is called insight (*vipashyana*). Insight is the natural and necessary complement to calm-abiding.

However, in an effort to stop the mind from wandering in meditation, practitioners sometimes forcibly try to suppress thoughts or create an artificial sense of calm. This is not calm-abiding. Trying to fabricate the nature of emptiness by simply blocking the mind is a mistake that can easily lead to a state of torpor. We should experience the union of appearances and emptiness. In doing so, we come to apprehend the ever-present pure awareness whether thoughts arise or not.

> To see perfectly the inconceivable absolute nature,
> Without any intellectual fabrications,
> Is an example of pristine wisdom.

We may have been introduced to the idea of the absolute nature by a teaching or the instructions of a qualified teacher. This idea is like an example that points at something but is not the thing itself. That is why Shechen Gyaltsap speaks of the "example of pristine wisdom"—something that is in tune with wisdom but is not wisdom itself. Once the teacher has pointed out the true nature of the mind, the next step is to remain in equanimity, unite with this understanding, and integrate it into our being so that it becomes a genuine realization. Only when we have a direct experience of the absolute nature, free of mental constructs, have we realized the pristine wisdom itself.

The Union of Calm-Abiding and Insight

> Beyond this, the supreme absolute wisdom—
> The field of understanding of the sublime beings
> Who have reached the state of unity,
> The meaning of the primordial union of insight—
> That brings about the wisdom and tranquillity of
> Remaining in the continuum of the natural state,
> Will be realized by the power of the guru's pith
> instructions.

The union of shamatha and vipashyana allows you to remain in the tranquillity of a mental state free from distractions and torpor while achieving a deeper insight into the true nature of mind.

Rely on the teacher's pith instructions to realize this wisdom of nondual calm-abiding and insight. These days people try to meditate according to instructions they read in books. However useful book knowledge may be, it will not bring you to the perfect wisdom. Just reading translations of the instructions or listening to tapes of the teachings will not be sufficient. But if you have devotion to your teacher and have made prayers of aspiration in the past, then you will realize the absolute nature through his instructions.

> Meditation experiences tainted by the notion of true
>   existence,
> Whether bliss, clarity, or nonthought,
> Are all deceptive and misleading.
> If you cling to things as real, you feed samsara
> And will never transcend the three worlds.

Try to remain free of the various meditative experiences that may arise, such as feelings of bliss, all-pervading clarity, or freedom from thoughts. These experiences will appear naturally, but if you cling to them, they can lead to rebirth in the three realms of samsara. Clinging to the reality of the experience of bliss will cause you to be reborn in the desire realm; clinging to clarity, you will be reborn in the form realm; and clinging to the absence of thoughts will lead to rebirth in the formless realm. Instead, strive to liberate yourself from samsara altogether and do not merely seek temporary happiness and bliss.

> Therefore, with consummate skill,
> Rest in simplicity, letting everything be
> In a state free of taking things as real,
> In which the one who realizes, the realized, and
>   realization
> Become inseparable, like pouring water into water.

> This is the fundamental nature beyond speech and
>   intellect,
> The definitive meaning, the transcendent perfection
>   of wisdom
> That can only be realized through one's own
>   awareness.
> Be determined to master this understanding!

If you are free of attachment to meditative experiences and can skillfully and naturally rest without contrivance according to the teacher's instructions, then you will experience the observing mind and what is observed as one. "Let everything be" does not mean force yourself to try to be complacent. That would be a dualistic concept. Instead, rest in simplicity, which is a state without fabrication.

Then that which is to be realized and the realization itself will all appear to merge, like pouring water into water. The watcher, the watched, and the watching are indivisible in the true nature of mind. Pure and direct awareness is the only way to understand this inexpressible nature, "the transcendent perfection of wisdom."

Establishing the Ultimate View and Meditation

> In brief, as the protector Atisha said,
> "Within the absolute, there are no distinctions;
> There are neither conditioned phenomena nor
>   absolute phenomena.
> In the face of emptiness, there are no distinctions,
>   none at all.
>
> "Realizing this without realization
> Is called simply 'seeing emptiness,'
> Seeing what cannot be seen.
> So it is said in the most profound sutras.
> Nothing to see, no one who sees,
> No beginning, no end,
> Peace.
>
> "Utterly beyond 'really there' and 'not really there,'
> Free of classification and reference point,
> It does not cease, does not remain,

Never comes, never goes;
It cannot be captured in words.

"It cannot be expressed; it cannot be viewed;
It never changes and has never ever existed as a solid
  reality.
The yogi who realizes this
Rids himself of the two veils: the veil of the
  obscuring emotions
And the veil covering all that is to be known."
So said Atisha in *Entering the Two Truths*.

Atisha explains that there is no essential division between relative and absolute truth, and likewise, no real difference between phenomena and their true nature. There are no distinctions within the nature of emptiness.

Ultimate reality cannot be perceived through concepts. We can, however, in an experiential way that transcends the ordinary conceptual mind, achieve a genuine understanding of reality as the union of appearances and emptiness.

There are two "veils" that obscure our true nature. "The veil of obscuring emotions" is formed by afflictive mental states such as desire, hatred, and jealousy. These states are the immediate cause of our sufferings in samsara. The second veil, the one that covers "all that is to be known," masks the understanding of the true nature of phenomena and of our own mind. Our attachment to believing in the existence of the phenomenal world and a personal self forms this veil, which is more subtle and difficult to dispel than the emotional veil.

A yogi who has relied on his teacher's instructions, analyzed his mind, and realized its ultimate nature will see "what cannot be seen," which is the true nature of things. Such a yogi is free of both the emotional and cognitive obscurations.

The Great Perfection and Devotion

> The eight qualities of understanding the ultimate
>   truth
> Are expounded in the sutras, and
> All this falls naturally into place in the Great
>   Perfection
> By pointing out the true nature of mind,
> Which is achieved through direct transmission
> Effected by the guru's blessings.

The *Prajnaparamita Sutra*[10] explains that "The eight qualities of understanding the ultimate truth" will naturally be present with realization of the Great Perfection. It can only be realized by a student with great perseverance, effort, and devotion, who keeps the precepts and practices under the guidance of an enlightened and compassionate teacher.

> This is not within the scope of ordinary minds,
> And those who are experts at discursive thought
> Will have no taste of it.
> "Absolute truth, arisen from itself,
> Is realized through faith alone."
> So it is said.

Experiencing the Great Perfection requires more than the mere cultivation of intellectual understanding or the study of many texts and books. Devotion to and deep confidence in an authentic spiritual teacher are necessary for this realization. Transmission of the understanding of the nature of mind can take place when an authentic, realized teacher and a disciple who sees the teacher as the Buddha himself come together in the right circumstances.

Direct transmission between guru and disciple does not necessarily need elaborate words and detailed instructions. There are examples of this in the life stories of the great masters. For example, Patrul Rinpoche and his longtime, close disciple, Nyoshul Lungtok, were lying in the meadow above Dzogchen Monastery in eastern Tibet one night.

Patrul Rinpoche asked, "Lungtok, do you know the nature of mind?"

The disciple replied, "Not really."

Then Patrul Rinpoche said, "Do you see the stars shining above in the sky?"

"Yes," Lungtok answered.

"Can you hear the dogs barking down near Dzogchen Monastery?"

"Yes."

Then the teacher asked, "How is the nature of mind?"

At that moment, Lungtok understood the absolute nature of mind. A pure connection between teacher and disciple can allow this to happen, so try to generate perfect devotion.

> Therefore hold on to the vital force of devotion
> That sees the guru as dharmakaya.
> Relax into unbroken pristine simplicity,
> And you will realize the essential meaning.

You cannot achieve spiritual accomplishment without devotion. In terms of qualities and achievements, your teacher is no different than the Buddha. But because your teacher is helping you at this moment, his kindness is even greater than that of all the buddhas of the past.

From the relative perspective, the guru appears in human form, turns the wheel of Dharma, and shows the path. Develop unchanging faith in your teacher and then merge your mind with his. By remaining in that state and maintaining the natural flow of awareness—perfect simplicity without any fabrication—you will realize the true nature of mind. Your mind will become one with your teacher's. At that point, from the absolute point of view, you will see him as the dharmakaya, the state of great evenness.

10

DEVIATIONS
FROM THE VIEW

If you miss this vital point
And complacently believe that you have not strayed
    into heretical deviations,
Or claim that you make no assertions,
Or cling to emptiness as a bare nothingness,
That is not the Middle Way.

If you fail to destroy the mental fixations
Of a materialistic point of view,
You have strayed even further from the Middle Way.
Therefore, foster freedom from clinging and all
    mental constructs.

The Middle Way is the indispensable foundation for realizing the Great Perfection. It is free from the extremes of nihilism and eternalism, from clinging to both emptiness and phenomena as solid. If you believe that emptiness just means eliminating all thoughts and getting rid of all phenomena without leaving space for the luminous quality of wisdom to shine, you are not following the authentic Middle Way.

If you have not fully realized the nature of emptiness and are merely adept at talking about it, you have not perfectly understood the Middle Way. Awareness and wisdom both have to be present. Just to talk about emptiness will not bring about the intimate realization of the view in your own experience.

> So-called great meditators who fail to realize this,
> Afraid that their practice will starve itself to death,
> Are zealously torturing themselves.
> What's the point of that?

Intellectual investigation can continue endlessly and fruitlessly like a small bird that flies off a ship in the middle of the ocean in an attempt to find the sky's limit. The sky is so vast that the bird will tire and have no choice but to return to the ship, failing to accomplish its goal. Similarly, we will never find an end to mental fabrications.

It is said, "If there is clinging, there is no view." Once we catch a glimpse of the absolute nature and stop clinging, we can fly through samsara, the world of existence, without fear or difficulty.

> What's the point of keeping track
> Of the comings and goings of thoughts?
>
> "Wakeful awareness that is beyond the
>   consciousnesses,"
> "Dharmakaya beyond the fundamental
>   consciousness,"
> "Freedom from the conditioned intellect,"
> I am sorry to say that none of these
> Are actually heard by ordinary beings
> And the meaning remains untapped,
> But I won't say too much about it.

All beings have tathagatagarbha
And thus they all possess the cause for buddhahood.
So view all of them as pure
And consider their great kindness.

Practitioners who make an endless effort to count their thoughts like mantras, yet fail to realize the union of appearance and emptiness, miss the point. Nor will they get very far just by being aware of the arising and ceasing of thoughts. Repeating what they have read or heard or trying to grasp these theories by mental concepts will not lead them to true understanding. These are not the correct ways to go about realizing that which is beyond intellect and concept. Shechen Gyaltsap says that he will "not say too much about it" because he is not writing a philosophical treatise. Rather, he is trying to convey his own deep experience as an indication to others on how to achieve it.

Find an authentic teacher, learn to be a good disciple, and most importantly, put your teacher's instructions into practice. The point is not simply to hang out with a teacher, but to achieve a true transformation that changes your attitude and makes you a better person. If you run after various teachers, practicing this and that without ever making a commitment, you will never deal directly with your afflictive emotions; they may even get worse. The Dharma is a teaching for self-transformation, not merely a form of entertainment.

Becoming jaded is one of the greatest pitfalls on the path. Once the teachings no longer permeate our awareness, the Dharma will not "work" as it should. To turn a stiff hide into supple leather, the Tibetans knead it with butter. Some hides remain hard even after they are constantly in contact with the butter. If we become complacent and do not genuinely try to change, we too will get "stiffer and stiffer" until we will resist any teachings we may hear.

See the Dharma in every experience. All sentient beings possess the buddha-nature, the tatagathagarba, and the cause of buddhahood. We must consider them with warmth and a kind heart. We progress on the path and cultivate loving-kindness, patience, and compassion as we learn to see other beings as pure. These qualities provide us with the necessary means to achieve buddhahood.

11

POSTMEDITATION: THE SIX
TRANSCENDENT PERFECTIONS

Between practice sessions,
Develop generosity and the other paramitas,
Without the three concepts.

Try to establish the nature of mind during meditation sessions. Do not stray into old habits and ordinariness between sessions. Instead, develop the six paramitas, or the six transcendent perfections. As they are free from the three concepts (the subject who acts, the object of the action, and the action itself) they can help us to create merit and wisdom.

GENEROSITY

Let's use the first paramita of generosity as an example of how this works. First, we rest in a state that is free from the notion of holding on to an "I" as the subject who performs the act of generosity. Second, we release any grasping at the object of generosity, the recipient of our help whose gratitude is usually expected. Last, there should be no grasping at the act of generosity itself. If we are completely free from these concepts, then we are practicing the true, or transcendent, generosity that can ferry us to the shore beyond samsaric existence.

There are different kinds of transcendent generosity. The first has to do with the giving of material things such as food, clothing, and other necessities with pure intention and no second thoughts, hidden agendas, or ulterior motives. Greater still is to give whatever we have, to surrender our most treasured possessions, or to give up clinging to our dearest friends or relatives. Beyond that, but only applicable to bodhisattvas who have truly realized the meaning of emptiness, there are no limits to what can be given. A bodhisattva at the first *bhumi* (stage of the path) will have no qualm or hesitation about sacrificing his limbs or even his life for the benefit of others.

The second kind of generosity is the gift of the Dharma. This also has various levels. For example, we can offer texts or funds so that people can study or enter the path. To make Dharma teachings available on a vast scale, thus benefiting all beings, is the best gift. This is what great masters do when they teach countless students.

The third type of generosity is to give protection from fear, to assist the sick and the destitute, to protect those in danger, and above all, to protect life. One way to do this is to buy animals before they are slaughtered or free fish that have been caught.

Of course, any act of generosity is extremely positive. However, transcendent generosity requires that we be free from strong clingings to the notion of "I" or the giver, the recipient, and the actual act of giving. Only then will our generosity be transcendent and help us to progress on the path of enlightenment.

DISCPLINE, PATIENCE, AND DILIGENCE

The second of the six paramitas is discipline, which also has three aspects. The first is to avoid the ten nonvirtuous acts. The second is to actively engage in the ten virtuous actions with an altruistic mind. The third aspect is to perform all actions for the benefit of others, thus creating incredible benefit for all.

The third paramita is patience, the complete abandonment of anger and ill will. It, too, has three main aspects. The first is to remain undisturbed by those who harm us in any way. We should maintain perfect forbearance and patience toward them, despite any ill treatment we might suffer.

The second aspect is to experience suffering with a positive attitude, using it to progress on the path and increase compassion. The great Kadampa masters said, "Your mind should be turned toward the Dharma; your Dharma practice should be turned toward becoming a renunciate. Your life as a renunciate should be focused on the thought of death, and your death should be focused on occurring in an empty cave." View this kind of renunciation and determination as a joy, not as a difficult burden.

The third aspect is to have patience toward the hardships of spiritual practice. Anything we encounter on the path, such as extreme heat or cold, should not hinder us. We need to have perfect patience and the capacity to endure anything without feeling upset. The ultimate aspect of patience is to accept the most profound meaning of the teachings without fear. Some people feel anguish simply thinking about emptiness. We need not feel frightened. In fact, we need to open fearlessly to the vast view in order to realize the meaning of emptiness.

The fourth paramita is diligence. In this case, diligence is the joy associated with striving toward a noble purpose. The first kind of diligence is like donning a suit of armor. You feel a strong determination that whatever circumstances occur, you will always follow the example of the great masters of the past with utmost determination and perseverance.

Second is the diligence of application, which is to dedicate all your strength to the immense task of Dharma practice. Do not feel that this is too difficult or that you can postpone it. Instead, determine to enter the practice immediately.

The third type of diligence is the diligence that is never satisfied, the feeling that you have never done enough. We often think, "Oh, this is certainly enough," when engaging in activities such as meditation, reciting mantras, or actively helping others for a short while. Instead of harboring this complacent thought, we should be like a hungry yak. When a yak is eating grass, its eyes are not looking at the grass it is eating, but at the grass further ahead. Similarly, we should never feel that we have done enough and should always look for new opportunities to practice. We need to make a constant effort until we reach enlightenment for the sake of all beings. Remember that to develop a stable concentration (*samadhi*) requires discipline. Without discipline, meditation will never progress.

CONCENTRATION

The fifth paramita is meditative concentration, or *dhyana*. There are three kinds of dhyana. The first leads to a state of ease and serenity, the second to the accomplishment of spiritual qualities, and the third to the direct benefit of others.

You need to avoid certain obstacles that can occur on the path to concentration. The first is to become enticed by spiritual experiences of bliss, lights, clarity, absence of discursive thoughts, and so forth. When this happens, you can mistakenly become like a child who, seeing lots of colorful things, gets absorbed in them. Do not give great importance to these meditative experiences. The second obstacle is to become attached to the experience of emptiness and to its ultimate meaning.

Once you have overcome these pitfalls, rest in equanimity in the ultimate nature of mind beyond discursive, conceptual thoughts. This is the genuine meditative concentration of the *sugatas*, or those who have realized the true nature of things.

Your mind should be neither too tense nor too lax when you

meditate. A mind that is tense and constricted can create a perfusion of thoughts that carries you into distraction. In contrast, a mind that is too relaxed has a tendency to sink into a torpor or even sleep. Avoid these two extremes and preserve a clear mindfulness whether your mind is in a state of distraction or falling into dullness.

In a continuous and balanced way, keep your mind focused on the object of concentration. Of course, thoughts will arise, but try not to give too much importance to them and allow them to vanish by themselves. Your concentration should be one-pointed, continuous, and lucid. Whenever it becomes too slack or too rigid, apply the proper antidote, and you will eventually develop a well-focused concentration.

While training in shamatha, you will progress through various levels of experience that eventually lead to a calmer mind. In the beginning, the mind is unruly and agitated. The idea of controlling thoughts seems as difficult as catching a writhing snake in your hand. When you try to stabilize the mind, it keeps running in all directions.

Normally, we do not pay attention to the condition of our minds. In effect, we do not realize how many thoughts we actually have. So as we start paying attention and try to sit quietly, we may have the sense that our thoughts are actually increasing. However, it is not our thoughts that are increasing, but our awareness of them. We are merely recognizing how agitated our mind has been all along. This state of mind can be compared to a rushing waterfall.

This restless, deluded mind creates and perpetuates all of our mental afflictions and sufferings, so we must develop a strong determination to tame it. As Shantideva said in the *Way of the Bodhisattva*, "There is no difficult task that cannot become easy if we persevere and become skillful through training."

Even when we pacify these wild thoughts and gross emotions,

we might still have cascades of thoughts that follow one another in a chain reaction. These thoughts are like a fast flowing stream cascading down a mountainside. Nonetheless, if we persevere in our meditation, fewer thoughts will arise and our mind will remain more peaceful and focused.

There are always many subtle, almost invisible thoughts creating a constant background static. Imagine looking at a big river in the distance. The water looks still. However, when you approach the banks, you will see that the river is moving, steadily flowing all the time. When this happens in your meditation, you will need to persevere in your training to maintain your concentration and progress. This is called familiarization.

When the subtle thoughts subside, you will have attained the stage of steadiness. You will be able to stay focused on the object of your meditation without any distraction. This is like an ocean that usually remains calm, except when disturbed occasionally by the wind. Although at this stage your mind can remain in calm concentration without mental constructs, noises, physical sensations, and so forth can still disturb the sense of peacefulness. If you continue to persevere and attain perfect concentration, the mind will effortlessly remain on any chosen object without difficulty, strain, or disturbance. It will remain vividly and clearly focused, and nothing will shake the calm. This is like a great mountain that cannot be shaken by winds.

During your training, various experiences may occur such as visions, feelings of bliss, and so on. Though a sign of progress, they are still tainted by ignorance and are not wisdom experiences. So whatever happens, never become infatuated with them; simply continue your training and your mind will become clear and serene. Your body will feel blissful and very light, almost as if it were puffs of cotton wool. These are the signs of purification and are indications that your training is progressing.

Wisdom

The sixth paramita is wisdom, of which there are also three types. The first is the wisdom born from study. The second is the wisdom that arises from profoundly reflecting upon the teachings and dispelling all doubts, confusions, misconceptions, and hesitations. In this process, you gain certainty about the meaning of all that you have heard or studied. The third wisdom is born from meditation. It can develop once you have this certainty. Try to integrate the teachings into your personal experience. This process will make them second nature. As a result, you will eventually realize the primordial wisdom. The main goal of the trainings on discipline and concentration is to increase wisdom.

Any practice you do should include the three steps of generating bodhichitta, practicing the six paramitas, and dedicating the merit. To practice free from the concepts of subject, object, and action and to dedicate any benefits to the good of all beings is to follow the excellent path that unites the accumulations of merit and wisdom.

PART THREE

VIRTUOUS
AT THE
CONCLUSION

12

DEDICATING THE MERIT

Dedicate everything toward great enlightenment.
Such is the excellent path uniting the two
    accumulations.
Thus the path of bodhichitta
In which both relative and absolute truths are one—
Emptiness with the essence of compassion—
Is the path that gladdens the Victorious Ones.

Meditate upon it continually and before long,
As the veils masking buddha-nature are cleared
    away,
You will earn the title of "enlightened one."

In essence, the path of bodhichitta is the way to actualize the primordial nature that is already present within us. Continuous meditation on the union of compassion and emptiness, characterized by great determination and perseverance, will soon clear away "the veils masking buddha-nature." These veils are the emotional veil created by the afflictive mental factors and the subtle cognitive veil that masks the understanding of the nature of all things and their multiplicity. These two veils prevent us from

achieving buddhahood. Once we remove them, we will see buddha-nature just as it is.

> Having actualized stainless, excellent qualities,
> Manifesting ceaseless, omnipresent, and
>   spontaneous buddha activity,
> You will act as a protector of all beings under the
>   skies.

Enlightenment is endowed with innumerable qualities that
manifest as all-encompassing compassion. "Spontaneous bud-
dha-activity" does not require any effort or particular intent. It
springs naturally from the compassionate wisdom of the buddhas. Through this ceaseless compassion, an enlightened being's
every action becomes beneficial to all beings.

COLOPHON

> Thus I, Padma Vijaya, having drunk the instructions
> that streamed forth from the mouths of the great lin-
> eage holders, have looked a little into them and now,
> having a little experience of them, at the request of a
> noble Dharma friend, I have spoken this short expla-
> nation.

> By this merit may the altruistic awakened mind
> Be born in the mind streams of all sentient beings.
> May they see the ultimate truth unveiled,
> The very face of buddha-nature.

In conclusion, the author summarizes the origin of his explanation, offers a prayer, and dedicates the merit of his work. I,
too, am very happy to have this opportunity to delve into and
explain this clear and beautiful text. You might have already been

familiar with these teachings. Although I had nothing extraordinary to add, I wanted to offer this book to you as a reminder.

According to the Tibetan tradition, there are three main types of commentaries: a literal, word-for-word commentary; a commentary on the meaning of the text; and an "all-encompassing" commentary. Here I have given a word-for-word commentary.

In this text, we studied different ways to develop bodhichitta. We need to gain real experience with these valuable instructions and integrate them into our lives. Doing so is the only reason to study them. The result of spiritual practice should be our inner transformation into better human beings. After practicing for months or years, we should be less prone to anger, pride, and jealousy. Our practice should lead us to a vaster, calmer mind.

For example, the whole point of dieting is to lose a few pounds, not to collect knowledge and become an expert on each and every diet. You may have heard about different diets and read many books, but you won't lose weight unless you put one of them into practice in your everyday life. Similarly, if you do not implement the teachings, your destructive emotions and self-clinging will not diminish. Then Dharma instructions will be of no use to you, no matter how many you receive.

Dilgo Khyentse Rinpoche always placed great emphasis on the importance of merging our mind with the Dharma and unifying the practice and daily life. Our aim should be to blend with the Dharma in meditation and to carry the quality of the meditation into all of our actions. Dharma needs to become second nature. We are probably not integrating the practice into our lives if, after having practiced a lot, we remain just as angry as before—or even a little more so. Another indication of a lack of integration is the absence of a sense of well-being. A genuine practitioner should at least become a good human being.

You might feel that you have some control of the mind or made some progress in your practice, yet as soon as difficulties confront you, the mental toxins overwhelm your mind with the same strength as before. If this happens, try to determine whether you are becoming a better human being or not. Are you slowly getting free of the obscuring emotions? Are you enjoying the fulfillment of inner freedom?

After years of practice, we should gain a sense of inner peace and become less vulnerable to outer circumstances. Masters like Patrul Rinpoche experienced great joy and profound happiness as a result of their Dharma practice. Inner freedom, relaxed and open happiness, and joy will arise when negative emotions and mental confusions disappear. In contrast, we will have missed the point of the practice if our mental poisons are still all-powerful, torment us constantly, and cause us to remain preoccupied with ourselves.

Although you may not have met Dilgo Khyentse Rinpoche or Shechen Gyaltsap, when you read their writings, you can experience the profundity of their understanding, the depth of their wisdom, and the vastness of their minds. This natural consequence of genuine Dharma practice is evident in practitioners whose practice is blossoming. Even those who have not yet achieved enlightenment still radiate a kind of inner well-being. This is the sign of a good practitioner. Someone with a weak practice can be difficult to be around. Such a person experiences many disturbing thoughts and problems without being able to handle them. In contrast, someone with a strong practice naturally becomes more open and experiences inner freedom. He or she is ready to tread the path of the bodhisattvas with joy, diligence, and compassion, benefiting others on the conventional as well as the ultimate level. May these teachings inspire a few to take these steps on the path to compassion and freedom with enthusiasm and confidence.

Notes

1. Respected and beloved by all schools of Tibetan Buddhism, Dilgo Khyentse Rinpoche (1910–1991) was one of the greatest masters of meditation and compassionate action in the last century. He was a brilliant scholar and poet whose writings fill twenty-five volumes. Many of his teachings have been published in English and other Western languages. The author is his grandson and Dharma heir. Shechen Gyaltsap, the author of this root text, was his first and main teacher. See Matthieu Ricard, *The Spirit of Tibet* (New York: Aperture, 2001).

2. Guru Rinpoche, or Padmasambhava, was predicted by the Buddha to be the one who would propagate the teachings of the Vajrayana. Invited to Tibet by the king Trisong Detsen in the eighth century, he succeeded in definitively establishing the Buddhist teachings of sutra and tantra in Tibet.

3. Patrul Rinpoche (1808–1887), born in eastern Tibet, was a highly accomplished master of the Nyingma tradition. He was famous for his nonsectarian approach and his extraordinarily humble and simple life. He was a prolific writer and is well known in the West as the author of *The Words of My Perfect Teacher*. See also note 6.

4. Quotation from Dilgo Khyentse Rinpoche in Matthieu Ricard, *Journey to Enlightenment*, (New York: Aperture, 1996), 33.

5. See *Introduction to the Middle Way*, trans. Pakmakara Translation Group, with commentary by Jamgön Mipham (Boston: Shambhala Publications, 2002), which is a translation of Chandrakirti's *Madhyamakavatara*.

6. Patrul Rinpoche, *The Words of My Perfect Teacher*, trans. Padmakara Translation Group (Boston: Shambhala Publications, 1994). This classic commentary on the preliminary practices of the Vajrayana includes detailed explanations of many aspects of the path. It discusses, with humor and clarity, the characteristics of authentic and inauthentic teachers.

7. The two obscurations are emotional obscurations, such as the afflictions of attachment and anger, and cognitive obscuration, or dualistic conceptual thinking—that prevents omniscience. These obscurations are like veils that cover the ultimate nature of the mind and phenomena.

8. The two wisdoms are the ability to discern correctly, usually with the particular sense of understanding of emptiness; and the primordial and nondual knowing aspect of the nature of the mind.

9. Shantideva, *The Way of the Bodhisattva*, trans. Padmakara Translation Group (Boston: Shambhala Publications, 1997).

10. The *Prajnaparamita Sutra* belongs to the second turning of the wheel of Dharma and expounds the doctrine of the emptiness of phenomena.

Glossary

ABSOLUTE TRUTH (Tib. *don dam bden pa*) The ultimate nature of the mind and the true status of all phenomena; the state beyond all conceptual constructs which can be known only by primordial wisdom and in a manner that transcends duality; the way things are from the point of view of realized beings.

ACTIONS (Tib. *las*) Actions that result in happiness for others are defined as positive, or virtuous; actions that give rise to suffering for others and oneself are described as negative, or nonvirtuous. Every action, whether physical, mental or verbal is like a seed leading to a result that will be experienced in this life or in a future life.

AFFLICTIVE MENTAL FACTORS, OR NEGATIVE EMOTIONS (Tib. *nyon mongs;* Skt. *klesha*) All mental events that are born from ego-clinging disturb the mind and obscure it. The five principal afflictive mental factors, sometimes called "mental poisons," are attachment, hatred, ignorance, envy, and pride. They are the main causes of both immediate and long-term suffering.

AGGREGATES, FIVE. *See* skhandas, five.

ALAYA-VIJNANA (Skt.; Tib. *kun gzhi,* lit. "the ground-of-all") According to the Mahayana, this is the fundamental and indeterminate level of the mind, in which karmic imprints are stored.

APPEARANCES (Tib. *snang ba*) The world of outer phenomena. Although these phenomena seem to have a true reality, their ultimate nature is emptiness. The gradual transformation of our way of perceiving and understanding these phenomena corresponds to the various levels of the path to enlightenment.

ARHAT (Skt.; Tib. *dgra bcom pa*) One who has vanquished the afflictive emotions, realized the nonexistence of a personal self, and thus is forever free of the suffering of samsara. Arhatship is the goal of the Shravakayana or Hinayana.

ASANGA (Skt.; Tib. *thog med*) A major figure in Mahayana Buddhism around 350 C.E.; the cofounder, with his brother Vasubandhu, of the Yogachara philosophy. He is the source of the Tradition of Vast Activities, which complements the Tradition of the Profound View stemming from Nagarjuna and Manjushri.

ATISHA (Skt.; Tib. *jo bo rje*) Also known as Dimpamkara Shrijnana (982–1054 C.E.); abbot of the Indian monastic university of Vikramashila. He came to Tibet at the invitation of the king Yeshe Ö to restore the buddha-dharma after its persecution by Langdarma. He introduced the Mind-Training teachings, which synthesize the bodhichitta traditions of Nagarjuna and Asanga.

AWARENESS, PURE (Tib. *rig pa*) The nondual ultimate nature of mind, which is totally free from delusion.

BODHICHITTA (Skt.; Tib. *byang chub kyi sems;* lit. "the enlightened mind") On the relative level, the wish to attain buddhahood for the sake of all beings, as well as the practices necessary to accomplish it: the path of love, compassion, the six transcendent perfections, and so on. On the absolute level, it is the direct insight into the ultimate nature of phenomena.

BODHISATTVA (Skt.; Tib. *byang chub sems dpa*) One who strives, through compassion, to attain full enlightenment or buddhahood for the sake of all beings.

BUDDHA (Skt.; Tib. *sangs rgyas*) One who has eliminated emotional and cognitive obscurations and has developed the two wisdoms to achieve enlightenment.

BUDDHA-NATURE, (Tib. *bde gshegs snying po*) The ultimate nature of mind, free from the veils of ignorance. Every sentient being has the potential to actualize this buddha-nature by attaining perfect knowledge of the nature of mind. It is, in a way, the "primordial goodness" of sentient beings.

CALM-ABIDING. *See* shamatha.

CHANDRAKIRTI (Skt.; Tib. *zla ba grags pa*) A sixth-century Indian master and author of unequaled dialectical skill. He followed the Madhyamika tradition of Nagarjuna. He is regarded as the systematizer and founder of the Prasangika subschool of Madhyamika.

CLINGING, GRASPING, OR ATTACHMENT (Tib. *bdag 'dzin*) Its two main aspects are clinging to the true reality of the ego and clinging to the reality of outer phenomena.

COMPASSION (Tib. *snying rje*) The wish to free all beings from suffering and the causes of suffering (negative actions and ignorance). This complements altruistic love (the wish that all beings may find happiness and the causes of happiness); sympathetic joy (rejoicing in others' qualities); and equanimity, which extends all three to all beings, whether friends, strangers, or enemies.

DHARMA (Skt.; Tib. *chos*) Usually used to indicate the doctrine of the Buddha. The "Dharma of transmission" refers to the corpus of oral or written teachings. The "Dharma of realization" refers to the spiritual qualities resulting from practicing these teachings.

DHARMAKAYA (Skt.; Tib. *chos sku*, lit. "dharma body") The emptiness aspect of buddhahood, which can also be translated as "body of truth" or "absolute dimension."

DHARMATA (Skt.; Tib. *chos nyid*) Thatness, the ultimate nature of phenomena, emptiness.

DUALITY, OR DUALISTIC PERCEPTION (Tib. *gnyis 'dzin*) The ordinary perception of unenlightened beings who see phenomena in terms of subject (consciousness) and object (mental images and the outer world) and believe in their true existence.

EGO, OR "I" (Tib. *bdag*) Despite the fact that we are a ceaselessly transforming stream, interdependent with other beings and the whole world, we imagine that there exists in us an unchanging entity that characterizes us and that we must protect and please. A thorough analysis of this ego reveals that it is only a fictitious mental construct.

EIGHT WORLDLY CONCERNS (Tib. *'jig rten chos brgyad*) The preoccupation with gain and loss, comfort and discomfort, good and evil reputation, praise and blame.

EMPTINESS (Skt. *shunyata;* Tib. *stong pa nyid*) The ultimate nature of phenomena, namely their lack of inherent existence. The ultimate understanding of emptiness is accompanied by the spontaneous arising of boundless compassion for sentient beings.

ENLIGHTENMENT (Tib. *sangs rgyas*) Synonymous with *buddhahood*. The ultimate accomplishment of spiritual training, when consummate inner wisdom is united with infinite compassion. A perfect understanding of the nature of mind and phenomena—their relative mode of existence (the way they appear) and their ultimate nature (the way they are)—is the fundamental antidote to ignorance and therefore to suffering.

ETERNALISM (Tib. *rtag par lta ba*) One of two extreme views (the other being nihilism); the belief in eternally existing entities such as a divine creator or the soul.

FOUR IMMEASURABLES OR FOUR BOUNDLESS ATTITUDES (Tib. *tshad med bzhi*) Four highly virtuous states of mind, regarded as immeasurable because they focus on all beings without exception and can produce infinite merits. They are loving-kindness, compassion, joy, and equanimity.

GODS (Tib. *lha;* Skt. *deva*) According to the Buddhist tradition, a class of beings—superior to humans—who although not immortal, enjoy immense power, bliss, and longevity.

GREAT PERFECTION (Tib. *rdzogs pa chen po;* Skt. *mahasandhi*) The summit of the nine vehicles and the ultimate view of the Nyingma school. Perfection means that the mind, in its nature, naturally contains all the qualities of the three bodies: its nature is emptiness, the dharmakaya; its natural expression is clarity, the sambhogakaya; and its compassion is all-encompassing, the nirmanakaya.

HINAYANA (Skt.; Tib. *theg dman;* lit. "Small Vehicle") The fundamental system of Buddhist thought and practice deriving from the first turning of the wheel of Dharma and centering around the teachings of the Four Noble Truths and the twelvefold chain of interdependent origination.

IGNORANCE (Tib. *ma rig pa*) An erroneous way to conceive of beings and things, which consists in attributing to them an existence that is real, independent, solid and intrinsic.

INTERDEPENDENCE, OR INTERDEPENDENT ORIGINATION (Tib. *rten cing 'brel bar 'byung ba*) A fundamental element of Buddhist teaching according to which phenomena are understood not as discrete existent entities, but as the coincidence of interdependent conditions.

KADAMPA (Skt.; Tib. *bka' gdams pa*) First of the schools of the New Tradition, which followed the teachings of Atisha. It stressed compassion, study, and pure discipline.

KALPA (Skt.; Tib. *bskal pa*) A cycle of formation and destruction of a universe. A great kalpa is divided into eighty intermediate kalpas. An intermediate kalpa is composed of one small kalpa during which the span of life increases and one small kalpa during which it decreases.

KARMA (Skt.; Tib. *las;* lit. "action") Refers to the law of cause and effect related to our thoughts, words, and behaviors. According to the Buddha's teachings, our destinies, joys, sufferings, and perceptions of the universe are due neither to chance nor to the will of some all-powerful entity; they are the result of previous actions. In the same way, our future is determined by the positive or negative quality of our current actions. Distinction is made between collective karma, which defines our general perception of the world, and individual karma, which determines our personal experiences.

KHARAK GOMCHUNG (GESHE) (Tib. *kha rag sgom chung*) An eleventh-century Kadampa lama who was famous for his perseverance and strict application of the teachings. It is said that he received the teachings of the Great Perfection and achieved the rainbow body.

LIBERATION (Tib. *thar pa*) Freedom from suffering and the cycle of existences. This is not yet the attainment of full buddhahood.

LOWER REALMS (Tib. *ngan song*) The hells and the realms of tortured spirits (*pretas*) and animals.

MAHAYANA (Skt.; Tib. *theg pa chen po;* lit. "Great Vehicle") The characteristics of Mahayana are the profound view of emptiness of the ego and all phenomena coupled with universal compassion and the desire to deliver all beings from suffering and its causes. To this purpose, the goal of Mahayana is the attainment of the supreme enlightenment of buddhahood, and the path consists of the practice of the six paramitas.

MEDITATION (Tib. *sgom*) A process of familiarization with a new perception of phenomena. Distinction is made between analytical meditation and contemplative meditation. The object of the former could be a point to be studied (for instance, the notion of impermanence) or a quality that the practitioner wishes to develop (such as love or compassion).

The latter allows the practitioner to recognize the ultimate nature of the mind and to remain within the realization of this nature, which lies beyond conceptual thought.

MERIT (Tib. *bsod names*) Positive energy arising from wholesome action or virtue (*dge ba*).

MIDDLE WAY (Tib. *dbu ma;* Skt. *madhyamika*) The teachings on emptiness first expounded by Nagarjuna and considered to be the basis of the Vajrayana. The word *Middle* indicates that this philosophy is beyond the points of view of the two extremes of nihilism and eternalism.

MIND (Tib. *sems*) In Buddhist terms, the ordinary condition of the mind as characterized by ignorance and delusion. A succession of conscious instants gives it an appearance of continuity. On the absolute level, the mind has three aspects: emptiness, clarity (the ability to know all things), and spontaneous compassion.

NAGARJUNA (Tib. *klu sgrub*) A first- to second-century Indian master who expounded the teachings of the Middle Way and composed numerous philosophical and medical treatises. He was the founder of the Madhyamika system of thought that is still regarded in Tibetan Buddhism as the summit of all philosophical systems.

NIHILISM (Tib. *chad par lta ba*) The extreme materialist view that considers the experiences of the physical senses to be the only reality and therefore denies the existence of past and future lives, the karmic principle of cause and effect, and so on.

NIRVANA (Skt.; Tib. *myang 'das;* lit. "beyond suffering") Various levels of enlightenment whose interpretation depends on whether they are considered from the Hinayana or the Mahayana point of view.

OBSCURATIONS (Tib. *sgrib pa;* Skt. *avarana*) Emotional obscurations (Tib. *nyon sgrib*) include afflictions such as attachment and anger; and cognitive obscuration (Tib. *shes sgrib*) is dualistic conceptual thinking, which prevents omniscience.

These two types of obscurations are like veils that cover the ultimate nature of the mind and phenomena.

PADMASAMBHAVA (Tib. *pad ma 'byung gnas,* lit. "lotus-born") Referred to by many other titles, including the Master of Orgyen and Guru Rinpoche. Invited to Tibet by the king Trisong Detsen in the eighth century, Padmasambhava succeeded in definitively establishing the Buddhist teachings of the sutras and tantra. He spread the Buddhist teaching of Vajrayana throughout Tibet and hid innumerable spiritual treasures for the sake of future generations. He is venerated as the Second Buddha, whose coming was predicted by the first, the Buddha.

PARAMITA (Skt.; Tib. *pha rol tu phyin pa*) A transcendent perfection or virtue, the practice of which leads to buddhahood and which therefore forms the practice of bodhisattvas. There are six paramitas: generosity, ethical discipline, patience, diligence, concentration, and wisdom. According to another reckoning, there are ten paramitas: the six already listed, as well as skillful means, strength, aspiration, and primordial wisdom. The last four are regarded as aspects of the wisdom paramita.

PATH (Tib. *lam*) The spiritual training that allows one to free oneself from the cycle of existence (samsara) and reach the state of buddhahood.

PATRUL RINPOCHE (Tib. *jigs med chos kyi dbang po*) A highly accomplished master (1808–1887) of the Nyingma tradition, from Eastern Tibet. He was famous for his nonsectarian approach and extraordinary simplicity of lifestyle. He was a prolific writer and is well known in the West as the author of *The Words of My Perfect Teacher,* an introduction to the practice of the Vajrayana.

PHENOMENA (Tib. *snang ba*) What appears to the mind through sensory perceptions and mental events.

PRAJNAPARAMITA SUTRA (Skt.; Tib. *shes rab kyi pha rol tu phyin pa*) The collection of sutras belonging to the second turning of the Dharma wheel and expounding the doctrine of shunyata, the emptiness of phenomena.

RELATIVE TRUTH (Tib. *kun rdzob bden pa*) The perception of phenomena as real on the level of ordinary experience.

SAMADHI (Skt.; Tib. *bsam gtan*) Meditative absorption of different degrees.

SAMSARA (Skt.; Tib. *'khor ba*) The wheel or cycle of existence; the state of being unenlightened in which the mind—enslaved by the three poisons of hatred, desire, and mental confusion—uncontrollably evolves from one state to another and passes through an endless stream of psychophysical experiences, all of which are characterized by suffering. It is only when one has realized the empty nature of phenomena and dispelled all mental obscurations that one can free oneself from samsara.

SANGHA (Skt.; Tib. *dge 'dun*) The community of Buddhist practitioners, whether monastic or lay. The term *noble sangha* refers to those members of the Buddhist community who have attained the path of seeing and beyond.

SECRET MANTRAYANA (Tib. *gsang sngags*) *See* Vajrayana.

SHAKYAMUNI The historical Gautama Buddha who attained full enlightenment beneath the bodhi tree in Bodhgaya, circa 500 B.C.E.

SHAMATHA (Skt.; Tib. *zhi gnas;* lit. "calm-abiding") Essentially a meditation in which the mind remains unmoving on an object of concentration. Although it is of great importance, this state is incapable of overcoming ignorance and the conception of a self.

SHANTIDEVA (Tib. *zhi ba lha*) A member of Nalanda University and the celebrated author of the *Bodhicharyavatara,* or *Way of the Bodhisattva.* He upheld the view of the Prasangika Madhyamika in the tradition of Chandrakirti. Shantideva was also the author of the *Shikshamuchchaya,* a valuable compendium of citations on discipline which would otherwise have been lost.

SKANDHAS, FIVE (Skt.; Tib. *phung po lnga*, lit. "heap" or "aggregate") The five skandhas are the component elements of form, feeling, perception, mental formations, and consciousness. These elements together create the illusion of "self" in the ignorant mind.

SUFFERING (Tib. *sdug bsngal*) The first of the Four Noble Truths, which are (1) the truth of suffering, which must be seen as omnipresent in samsara; (2) the truth of the origin of suffering, which are the negative emotions that we must eliminate; (3) the truth of the path (spiritual training) that we must take in order to reach liberation; and (4) the truth of the cessation of suffering, the fruit of training, or the state of buddhahood. There are three types of suffering (Tib. *sdug bsngal gsum*) (1) The suffering of suffering—pain as such; (2) the suffering of change—the fact that happiness is impermanent and liable to turn into suffering; and (3) all-pervading suffering in the making—the fact that all actions grounded in the ignorance of the true nature of things will sooner or later bring forth suffering.

SUGATA (Skt.; Tib. *bde bar gshegs pa*, lit. "one who has gone to, and proceeds in, bliss") An epithet for a buddha.

SUTRAS (Skt.; Tib. *mdo*) The words of the Buddha, which were transcribed by his disciples.

TANTRA (Skt.; Tib. *rgyud*, lit. "continuum") The texts of Vajrayana Buddhism, which expound the natural purity of the mind. The Nyingma school classifies the tantras into outer tantras (Kriya, Upa, and Yoga) and inner tantras (Mahayoga, Anuyoga, and Atiyoga). The Sarma, or new translation, tradition uses another method which divides the tantras into four classes: Kriya, Upa, Yogatantra, and Anuttaratantra.

TATHAGATA (Skt.; Tib. *de bzhin gshegs pa,* lit. "one who has gone thus") An epithet for the Buddha.

TATHAGATAGARBHA (Skt.; Tib. *de gshegs snying po*) The potential for buddhahood; the luminous and empty nature of the mind.

THOUGHTS, DISCURSIVE (Tib. *rnam par thog pa*) An ordinary linking together of thoughts conditioned by ignorance and relative reality.

THREE DOORS OF LIBERATION (Tib. *rnam thar sgo gsum*) A central notion of the Mahayana teachings of the second turning of the Dharma wheel. They are a means of approaching ultimate reality through an understanding of three qualities implicit in all phenomena. The three doors are (1) all phenomena are empty; (2) they are beyond all attributes; and (3) they are beyond all aspiration or expectation.

THREE JEWELS (Tib. *dkon mchog gsum;* Skt. *triratna*) The Buddha, the Dharma, and the Sangha.

THREE KINDS OF WISDOM The wisdom resulting from hearing, reflecting on, and meditating on the teachings.

THREE POISONS (Tib. *dug gsum*) The three negative emotions of hatred, desire, and mental confusion.

TRADITION OF THE PROFOUND VIEW (Tib. *lta ba zab mo'i lugs*) The sutras of the second turning of the Dharma wheel, setting forth the profound view of emptiness, were compiled by Manjushri and commented upon by Nagarjuna. With regard to the ritual for taking the bodhichitta vow and its ensuing practice, the Nyingmapas mostly follow the tradition of Nagarjuna. With regard to their view, however, they follow both the Tradition of the Profound View and the Tradition of Vast Activities taught by Asanga.

TRADITION OF VAST ACTIVITIES (Tib. *spyod pa rgya che ba'i lugs*) The bodhisattva Maitreya compiled the sutras of the third turning of the wheel, composed the five treatises named after him (which establish the view of "emptiness of other," or *gzhan stong*), and taught them to Asanga. Asanga also wrote *Five Treatises on the Grounds* and other works. His brother Vasubandhu, after embracing the Mahayana, wrote many works of which *Thirty Stanzas on the Mind* is the most outstanding. These are the source of the Tradition of Vast Activities, which expounds the teaching on the buddha-nature, the bodhisattva bhumis, and so on. Atisha introduced this tradition's ritual of the vow and practice of bodhichitta to Tibet.

TRIPITAKA (Skt.; Tib. *sde snod gsum*) The three collections of the words of the Buddha (*Vinaya, Sutra,* and *Abhidharma*).

TWO OBSCURATIONS, OR TWO VEILS. *See* obscurations.

VAJRASATTVA (Skt.; Tib. *rdo rje sems dpa'*) The buddha who embodies the Hundred Families. The practice of Vajrasattva and recitation of his mantra are particularly effective for purifying negative actions.

VAJRAYANA, OR THE SECRET MANTRAYANA (Skt.; Tib. *rdo rje theg pa*) The body of teachings and practices, based on the tantras and scriptures, that center on the primordial purity of the mind.

VIPASHYANA (Skt.; Tib. *lhag mthong;* lit. "enlarged vision" or "profound insight") The primordial wisdom that overcomes the ignorant belief in the existence of self and realizes ultimate reality.

WISDOM (Tib. *shes rab;* Skt. *prajna*) (1) The ability to discern correctly, usually with the particular sense of understanding of emptiness. (2) (Tib. *ye shes:* Skt. *jnana*) The primordial and nondual knowing aspect of the nature of the mind.

YOGI, OR YOGINI (Tib. *rnal 'byor pa* or *rnal 'byor ma*) Someone who practices yoga; a spiritual practitioner. *Yogi* is male; *yogini* is female.